PRAISE FOR *GRIEVING ROOM*

"In *Grieving Room*, Leanne Friesen offers us a rare and wonderful gift: a story of loss that is both vulnerable and strong, raw and wise. With the compassion of a pastor and the precision of a fellow griever, Friesen points us toward a path of healing, with all its ups and downs, mountains and valleys. I will be recommending this book for years to come."

—**Amanda Held Opelt**, songwriter and
author of *A Hole in the World*

"Having suffered great loss and experienced profound grief as a teen, I didn't have many resources to help me navigate all I was feeling. Not anymore. Leanne Friesen is doing inspiring work by normalizing conversation surrounding grief and creating resources for the grieving community with this honest, firsthand account of how she made space for her own grief. This book is a great gift for a grieving friend or loved one when we just don't know what to do or say to help. Thank you, Leanne, for your bravery and honesty in writing this book."

—**TJ Jackson**, founder of Dee Dee Jackson Foundation

"A poignant and thoughtful must-read for grievers. This book is a gift for anyone traversing life after loss."

—**Sally Douglas**, coauthor of
Good Mourning: Honest Conversations

"In this remarkable book, Leanne Friesen wraps up a treasure trove of unconventional wisdom in deeply personal and poignant stories of people dealing with grief (including herself), and the result is a rare work that is as emotionally compelling as it is intellectually insightful. All of us will sooner or later experience extreme grief and will be called upon to help others in various stages of grief—which is why I believe everybody reading this endorsement would benefit greatly by reading *Grieving Room*."

—**Greg Boyd**, pastor, theologian, and author

"This book is a cozy cabin in the woods, welcoming you in after a cold and lonely journey of grief. Take your time with these pages; don't rush through them. Your heart will steadily open up and receive healing from the chaotic, complicated combination of both intense pain and joy over having lost someone after loving them so deeply."

—**Lydia Sohn**, writer and United Methodist pastor

"*Grieving Room* reminds us to take the work of grieving seriously. It is a patient, kind, deeply personal and wise work of spiritual direction through the rooms of grief. On behalf of pastors, chaplains, and the rest of us who must all walk these paths of loss, much thanks to Leanne Friesen for this extraordinary gift."

—**David Fitch**, author and B. R. Lindner Chair of Evangelical Theology at Northern Seminary

"If you are experiencing the pain of loss, you want a companion who understands what you are going through. With honesty, eloquence, and humor Leanne Friesen tells the story of her own grief journey. As a wise and expert guide, she can help you find your own path to healing. I deeply respect and trust Leanne and highly recommend this book. You are not alone."

—**Mark A. Scandrette**, author of *Belonging and Becoming* and *The Ninefold Path of Jesus: Hidden Wisdom of the Beatitudes*

GRIEVING ROOM

GRIEVING ROOM

MAKING SPACE FOR ALL THE HARD THINGS
AFTER DEATH AND LOSS

LEANNE FRIESEN

BROADLEAF BOOKS
MINNEAPOLIS

Library of Congress Cataloging-in-Publication Data

Names: Friesen, Leanne, author.
Title: Grieving room : making space for all the hard things after death and
    loss / Leanne Friesen.
Description: Minneapolis, MN : Broadleaf Books, [2023] | Includes
    bibliographical references.
Identifiers: LCCN 2023014709 | ISBN 9781506492377 (hardback) | ISBN
    9781506492384 (ebook)
Subjects: LCSH: Grief. | Death--Psychological aspects.
Classification: LCC BF575.G7 F75 2023 | DDC 155.9/37--dc23/eng/20230516
LC record available at https://lccn.loc.gov/2023014709

Cover design: Faceout

Print ISBN: 978-1-5064-9237-7
eBook ISBN: 978-1-5064-9238-4

Printed in China

In loving memory of
Andrea Caines (1980–2015)
Stephanie (Caines) McIntyre (1976–2021)
Dana Caines (1973–2022)
Christine (Newhook) Eddy (1970–2021)
and, of course, Roxanne Howse (1965–2013):
cherished cousins of one generation whom cancer took too soon.

AUTHOR'S NOTE

In order to honor the personal nature of many of the accounts used in this book, a number of names and identifying details have been changed, in consultation (when possible) with those involved. I also wish to affirm that I sought permission, when possible, to share the stories used in this work (even in cases where details are changed), in recognition that these stories are not just my own.

My faith, as a Christian pastor, is interwoven with my own experience of grieving. I recognize this will not be the case for all of you who read this book, and I have tried to write about these experiences in a way that will make sense to everyone, whether or not you identify with the Christian faith. If the biblical accounts do not resonate with you, please feel free to consider the themes I tried to share through those stories from your experience. All Scripture passages are from the New International Version unless otherwise stated.

CONTENTS

CONTENTS

INTRODUCTION

A lot of us don't know what to do with grief. We often think that the best thing to do with grief is to avoid it. We say things like "Time heals all wounds!" and "Let's try to think positive!" When someone is struggling longer than we think they should, we encourage them to "move on" or question why they aren't "over" their loss just yet. We think we are helping when we tell grievers that the person they loved is "in a better place" or "they wouldn't want you to be sad."

Encouraging people to look on the bright side? We're good at that. Trying to help people feel better? That makes sense to us. Looking for ways to "get over" a loss? We assume this is the goal.

What makes less sense to us is giving grief room, which is hard. But that's what grief most often needs.

In 2013 my sister Roxanne died of melanoma. Of all the things that people said to me during her dying, one stands out to me most: the words spoken by a well-meaning person hoping to comfort me. I don't remember who said these words, though I know it was a woman. I don't remember what day they were said, though I can picture exactly where I was standing when I heard them. I remember what I was wearing, what the weather was like that day, and the sound of the people buzzing around us as we talked. And I only have to pause for a moment to relive the confusion I felt as I processed what was happening.

My sister was nearing the final days of her life after eight years of living with cancer. She had stopped treatments, planned her funeral, and made arrangements for palliative care. It had been several days since she had been coherent, weeks since she had been without pain. My whole family was already grieving, and I was smack-dab in the middle of the trauma of the slow, painful death of a sibling, one that I could barely process.

At the church where I work as a pastor, I was mingling with congregants in the lobby after our Sunday service. As happened often in those days, someone asked me how Roxanne was doing. I started to answer: "Well, she's dying—"

With a mixture of horror and dismay, this person put her hand over her mouth. "Don't say that!" she said vehemently.

I was temporarily stunned, shocked by her statement and confused by how I should respond. "What do you want me to say?" I asked, utterly bewildered.

"Well, it's just . . . you have to have *hope!*" the woman said.

I debated walking away and taking my aching soul with me, but I wanted to defend myself. I wanted this woman to understand why I absolutely needed to say what I had said. "I *do* have hope," I answered, trying to keep my emotions in check. "I have hope that if we live, we live to the Lord and if we die, we die to the Lord, and that whether we live or die, we belong to the Lord." My voice stayed surprisingly even as I shared this favorite Scripture that had brought me hope during this painful season. And maybe now it would help her get the hint to back down a bit?

"But you can't *give up!*" the woman pressed on, clearly distraught.

I don't remember what I said next. But I remember that I was baffled, and I was hurt. What did this person even mean? What did "not giving up" look like? Was it praying for a miracle that I had accepted was not going to happen in this lifetime? Was it refusing to admit that my sister's death was imminent? Was it reciting platitudes like "She can still beat this," or pretending, for this woman's sake, that Roxanne's health was better than it was? How was it "giving up" to accept the reality that my sister was going to die?

I heard the message loud and clear on that Sunday in the spring of 2013: There is no space for your grief here. There is no space for death. There is no room for your despair.

The woman was okay with miracles. She was comfortable with optimism. She could make sense of one version of hope. But death? Not so much.

I know she meant well and that she was only trying to protect me from the pain that my sister dying would cause me. Suggesting that the death might not happen was meant to uplift me. But in that moment, I needed space for a pain that wasn't going anywhere anytime soon. I needed to name the huge thing that was right in front of me: the thing that consumed all my waking thoughts and kept me up at night. I didn't need to be told to "not give up." I didn't need to be told to "have hope." I needed grieving room. In a culture of relentless optimism, I was learning that this space was going to be hard to find.

In the days and years that followed—as my sister died, and then as I grieved, and then as I supported others who were grieving—I found that the need for grieving room was not unique to me. Nor was the struggle to find it particularly rare. Grieving room is endangered in a culture that thinks it is more helpful to rush past grief than lean into it. The message a lot of grieving people hear is similar to that one statement I heard in a church lobby from someone who wanted to help me. Your sister is dying? "Don't say *that!*"

Maybe you've heard it too, in one form or another. Maybe you've shared with someone that you're feeling hopeless after a miscarriage. Or that you are devastated by the death of your spouse. Or that you don't know how to make sense of living as an orphan after losing both your parents. And some way or another, you've been told that your feelings aren't quite right. You should stay optimistic, or be thankful for the time you had, or celebrate that they had a long life. "Don't say that!" takes a lot of forms.

You're sad that your loved one died? *Everything happens for a reason!* It's been a few months and you're still grieving? *Perhaps it's time to move on* . . . You're angry about the terrible thing that happened to you? *At least it wasn't any worse!*

Many of us simply don't know how to make room for grief. The truth was I didn't know how to give this room either, not even to myself. I learned about grieving room as I grieved. I learned it at my sister's deathbed. I learned it on long nights of wailing for my sister and a life cut short. I learned it as I mourned for a person I loved in the months and years after she died.

Through this, I discovered what it meant to give grieving room to others. My job as a pastor puts grieving people in my life all the time, and I see now what they most need is exactly what I did: space for their grief. I am learning to give grieving room at gravesides and funeral homes; in my office, over a dwindling box of Kleenex; or in a widow's overly warm living room as she laments the loss of a husband of sixty years. Over and over I sit with people trying to make sense of their grief, people who don't need me to fix or rush or heal them. They need me to help them give their grief room.

This book is a culmination of lessons learned from loss. I tell the story of one little sister who lost a big sister too soon and who had to learn the hard way that there is no skipping, avoiding, or going around grief. My story is not unusual. It is simply mine. It is not the same story that Roxanne's children or her husband or my parents or Roxanne's friends would tell. We each only have one piece of the story, and this one is mine. My piece taught me about grieving room.

I hope this story can help you. I hope it will give the grieving—and those who love them—permission to give sorrow the space it needs.

I am four years old. I am sitting in my big sister Roxanne's room, a small space carved into our unfinished basement, which she has painted yellow with a giant black "Roxy" in cursive writing on the wall. Roxanne is packing because she is moving away to go to university. She explains that she will come and visit, of course, and she says she will miss me, her little sister. I feel sad that she is leaving. But she has made room for me in this time of change, room to help me understand.

I am seven years old. Roxanne has brought me a book called *The Paper Bag Princess*. She knows about this book because she's studying to be a teacher, and so she knows all the best things. She reads it to me, doing the perfect voice for each character. She has the most hilarious dragon voice. Later I tell her to tell me and my cousin the story again. We don't have the book, but Roxanne tells the story anyway. Her dragon voice is still perfect. My cousin and I laugh and laugh. There is so much room around her lap, so much room for children, for stories, for delight.

I am seven and nine and ten and twelve, and Roxanne has returned from Scotland or England or Israel or Turkey. She has brought me a t-shirt from Istanbul or a music box from Switzerland, a wallet from Crete or a Loch Ness monster sculpture from Scotland. She is the coolest. I can hardly wait to brag to my friends about what she brought me. Tell them how she lived on a kibbutz. That she went to Troy. That she has seen the world. No one has a sister like her. I want to be just like her when I grow up. I want to always have room for more adventure.

I am twenty-two and I've just moved to the same city as Roxanne after finishing my degree. It's a Tuesday, so it's our weekly dinner together at her house. Her daughters are four and two. After dinner it is time for a concert because she wants her girls to feel confident playing their instruments for others. We listen again to the cranks of the kids' violins, clapping wildly after each performance. Roxanne beams with joy. There is always room for her children in her busy life, never time she won't give them.

I'm twenty-four, and I've just gotten home after being out with friends. I'm living with Roxanne and Mike in between leases. They never mind. Roxanne and Mike are watching TV in their room. As always, they tell me to come on in. I snuggle in beside Roxanne as we watch the end of *Survivor*. Even now that she is married, there's still room for me.

I am thirty-one and we are gathered around the piano, ready to sing as my niece Hannah plays. As usual, we start with the musical theater song book. We sing "I Don't Know How to Love Him" from

5

Les Misérables. Roxanne tells us again about seeing it live in London in its first production and comments as usual to her daughter Emily that she would make a perfect Éponine. We move on to the hymns. We belt out "Amazing Grace" in harmony. There is room for song after song after song.

I am thirty-two and I have just given birth to my second child, a little girl. We have already decided to name my daughter Lucy Roxanne. When we phone Roxanne to tell her, she says, "Now this is the second time I've cried today." The first was after she had watched the movie *Toy Story 3*. There is barely room for all the joy.

There is always room. Room for anyone who needs a friend. Room for someone else at her table. Room for me to stay at her house. Room for her kids to have all her heart. Room to laugh, and laugh, and laugh.

And then suddenly I am thirty-five and she is lying in a hospice bed on an unseasonably warm May night. She is covered in tumors. Her hair is gone. Her body is broken. And she breathes one more time before I realize she will not breathe again.

How can there ever be room for happiness in the world again? How could there ever be enough room for the grief that I feel? This is what I will have to learn.

Perhaps you need to learn it too: You, with your own snapshots, your own memories, your own devastation. You, figuring out what room for grief looks like when loss looms large over your own life. You, wondering how to support a friend or family member who has been leveled by immense loss. You know what it is to wonder how life can continue when grief is all consuming. You also need grieving room.

1

ROOM TO BE UNCERTAIN
WHEN YOU BELIEVE AND DON'T BELIEVE AT THE SAME TIME

If you're trying to get your first job as a pastor, preaching about not having enough faith might not be a great idea. But in May 2005, that's what I did. After what had happened in the weeks prior to my sermon, it was the only message I knew how to give.

It started when Roxanne picked me and my husband, Dallas, up from the airport to drive us home for my grandmother's funeral. I had grown up in a small village in Newfoundland, Canada, but in my mid-twenties had decided to study at a seminary in Hamilton, Ontario, literally a thousand miles away. I didn't know much about seminary. I knew it was a place where you could study the Bible, and I wanted to do that. I didn't know that it would lead to me deciding to become a pastor nor that I would meet my husband there. I didn't know that Hamilton would become home.

On that day in April 2005, there was still a lot I didn't know. I didn't know that what I would remember most about that week would not be my grandmother's funeral. I didn't know that the pain of losing her would pale in comparison to the pain that was coming. I was blissfully unaware of the significance of one little statement, one that seemed to mean nothing and that I would only remember when it came back to haunt us later.

It was unusual for only Roxanne to meet us at the airport in Newfoundland. Normally, trips home meant the entire family came to meet us as we descended the escalator toward baggage claim. But my grandmother had died only the day before, and my parents were busy. Roxanne, who lived in St. John's nearer to the airport, would pick us up and drive us to my parents' house, an hour from the city. My brother, Jason, who lived on the other side of Newfoundland, was heading to our parents that day as well. My sister Deanne, who lived with her family across the country in British Columbia, was not able to come home for the funeral.

I didn't mind that Roxanne was the only one to meet us. Seeing her at the bottom of the stairs instantly made me feel at home. I hugged her petite frame, bundled up in winter clothes, returned her huge smile, saw again her trademark dimple on the left side of her face, the one that was especially pronounced because of a tooth removed when she was a child. The gap in her teeth never kept her from smiling, though, which she did that day, as she flicked her short brown hair out of her eyes and welcomed us home.

I knew we would be seeing a lot of each other over the next week. Her house in St. John's, where she lived with her husband, Mike, and her two girls, then eight and six years old, felt as much a home to me as the house I grew up in. Although I was keenly feeling the loss of my beloved Granny, I also was looking forward to days at Roxanne's house—days I knew would include trips to the mall, lunch dates, board games, lengthy suppers in her dining room, show-tune sing-alongs around her piano, and laughing until our sides hurt. As Roxanne hugged us welcome, it felt so very good to be home.

So it didn't even occur to me to be worried when she said it. We had just gotten into her car and pulled onto the almost empty highway that stretched to our parents' home in Trinity Bay when she said, "I'm not actually sure I should be driving. I had this thing removed from my head today and I'm actually feeling a little off center."

"What did you have removed from your *head*?" I said, laughing.

"Oh, I've had this little thing on my head for a few months, and Dave thought I should get it removed, so he removed it this morning." Dave was a good friend of Roxanne's and, conveniently, a doctor.

"So basically you had head surgery today?" I said.

"Pretty much," she laughed back.

We joked about it a lot over the next few days. The cut to remove the growth on her head had been deep, so Roxanne often felt the impact of the minor procedure. She would stand up and feel light-headed; "Oh, that's your head surgery," we would tease. If she mixed up words or forgot something, we'd blame the "head surgery."

Looking back, I am shocked that none of us felt cause for alarm. We are a family of worriers. We naturally prepare for the worst-case scenario. But for some reason, we didn't fret. We didn't worry that her friend (a *doctor*) had seen the growth on Roxanne's head and recommended it be removed. Didn't register that he had "squeezed her in" his schedule quickly because he felt it shouldn't wait. Didn't feel anxious that she had had this for *several months* and that it had grown. With all these things named before us, somehow, we didn't worry.

In that week of farewelling my beloved grandmother, we never asked: What *is* on your head, Roxanne? Why is Dave so worried? Why *did* he have to cut so deep that it made you light-headed for a few days? For a week, the mysterious bump on Roxanne's head was a punchline instead of a problem.

I was back in Hamilton before we learned that the funny little growth wasn't funny after all. The phone rang early one morning, with Mike's voice on the other line. The test results were back. It was cancer, at least stage two melanoma and likely far worse. Roxanne was scheduled for invasive surgery in three weeks. There were lots of questions about how much the cancer had already spread and what treatments would be needed.

How had we not known? Why hadn't we been more worried? How had we been so flippant? I was haunted by all the jokes we had made, all the signs we had missed that this was serious. And I carried a deep, underlying terror that perhaps there had been another sign that I had missed that something was awry: a dream I had had a few weeks before, before my grandmother died and before any news of head surgeries or cancer had turned our lives inside out.

I have never had a dream like it, before or since. In the dream, Roxanne had died. I didn't remember details, except the certainty of her death. The only other thing that I had recalled, upon waking, was that a song was playing, one that was popular in my church at the time called "Jesus, All for Jesus," a song about accepting God's will as the way to freedom.

I had been so unnerved by that dream that it had taken me hours to get over it. My husband had found me wide awake early in the morning, still crying. He'd helped me calm down a little, kept telling me it was just a dream. I had been able to mostly forget about it—until two weeks later, when I heard Roxanne had cancer and the dream came flooding back to me.

Now I couldn't stop thinking about the dream. A dream that Roxanne had died. A dream where a song kept saying: "It's only in your will that I am free." Had God been telling me Roxanne would die? Had God been sending me a warning, a prophecy, a preparation?

The thought petrified me so much that I couldn't bring myself to tell anyone my deepest fear: that God had sent me a dream to prepare me for Roxanne's death. I carried an aching dread inside me, refusing to burden anyone else with my own anxiety, as we waited for Roxanne's surgery date.

And then, in the midst of this, I had to preach a sermon. It wasn't just any sermon but the first sermon I would share at a church as they decided whether to hire me as their new pastor. As the final phase of a pastoral search process that had been ongoing for several months, I would "preach for the call": present a sermon summarizing my deepest convictions, so the church could decide if I was the right fit for them. It is a very intimidating form of a job interview, with 150 people collectively deciding your fate.

Although it was scary, it was also exciting because everything about this call seemed too good to be true. I was only twenty-seven years old and fresh out of school. I was joining a new denomination. My husband was also being considered for the role of associate pastor at the same congregation. A church where we could work together, so soon after graduation, in the city we were already living? It was beyond anything we could have hoped for.

But first I had to preach a sermon, which was slated to happen just a few days before Roxanne's surgery.

The idea of starting in this role had already been overwhelming, but as I prepared that sermon, I second-guessed myself even more. Roxanne's diagnosis, and how I felt about it, had jarred me. At that point I believed it was my job to have enough faith that God would heal Roxanne. *I* had to believe enough in order for her cancer to get better. If *I* didn't believe enough, then Roxanne could not be healed. Her healing rested on the shoulders of my faith, I thought, and I was petrified it was insufficient. I had absorbed a form of Christianity that taught me that faith is something you work really, really hard at in order to please God. Three years of seminary had not adequately challenged that view, even when my sister's life was at stake. I was scared, unsettled, and worried that I did not have enough faith that God would heal my sister.

What kind of pastor would that make me? What kind of *sister*?

When people come to God with a big request, some will ask: "Do you have enough faith for your healing?" We see this on television with faith healers all the time. This idea may seem foreign to you, depending on how you grew up, but some of us have been deeply shaped by this question. Because of it, if healing does happen, we congratulate ourselves. If it doesn't, we feel like we failed. We assume it's because we didn't believe enough. We didn't pray enough. We didn't trust enough.

I lived most of my life not having to face this question in a practical way, but now it plagued me. *Did* I have enough faith for God to heal Roxanne? It seemed like I didn't. I was not a good "having a sister who may be dying" person. I was not calm or peaceful. I was anxious, worried, and harried. Basically, I was a mess.

About this time, I revisited a story that I had known for many years but never really considered much before. It's a story about the healing of a boy, and it's found in the Bible in a book called Mark. In this passage, Jesus and three of his closest friends have just had an incredible spiritual experience on the top of a mountain. When they return from this incident, they find Jesus's other followers caught up in some sort of argument. When Jesus asks what is happening, a man from the crowd explains that he brought his son, who is "possessed by a spirit," to Jesus's followers to be healed, but they couldn't do it. Most scholars now think that this boy had some sort of seizure disorder, understood as a spiritual condition at the time. Whatever his ailment, we have a man who has a sick son that he can't help. And now Jesus's followers couldn't fix him either.

When Jesus enters the scene, he asks what is going on and then asks to see the boy. The father is still hopeful and still desperate. He says to Jesus, "If you can do anything, take pity on us and help us." Jesus answers, "If you can? Everything is possible for one who believes!"

To this I say: *ouch.*

This story was hard to read in those days of my uncertainty. It seemed to affirm every fear I had. It said that anything was possible for the one who has enough faith. That meant that if Roxanne didn't get better, it must be because my faith was insufficient. I needed to muster up more faith to ensure Roxanne was healed, just like the man needed to have more faith for his son. That was what I was telling myself.

But what I hadn't noticed until the spring of 2005 was that these words of Jesus were not the end of this story. In fact, the next line in the narrative is not only one of the best lines in the story; in my opinion, it is one of the best moments in the whole Bible. In the next line, the father says, "I do believe. Help me overcome my unbelief."

That statement is so perfect that it still makes me laugh out loud a little every time I read it. Isn't that all of us, no matter what faith we hold or don't hold? We believe—but also, we don't. We have faith—but not enough. We pray—but also, we're not sure there's any point in doing so. Even if we put no value in prayer and have no interest in reaching out to any form of a God for help, most of us will likely resonate with the mixed-up emotions of really hoping for the best while also being terrified the worst will happen. "I do believe. Help me overcome my unbelief"—it is a universal prayer. And it was exactly how I felt.

I realized what I needed to preach about. With all the nerve of a young preacher embracing a theology she has not yet lived, I preached about coming to Jesus with this kind of quaky, not-quite-sure-but-trying-really-hard faith. I talked about the surprising paradox of what the Bible tells us it means to believe and "not doubt" while also teaching us that it's God who helps us believe. I talked about how faith is not something we muster up for ourselves but rather something that God gives us when we don't think we have enough.

"I am scared," I told a room of strangers, "that my sister will die. And I am asking God to give me faith to have more faith." I told them that I was learning that it wasn't my job to have a perfect faith. Instead, I had to start by bringing Roxanne to Jesus, one shaky step at a time.

I said all this in my very first sermon to what would become my church for the next eighteen years. I pointed out that this father in Scripture, with his flip-floppy faith, was loved by Jesus. That Jesus never chastised him or told him he wasn't good enough. He said, "Bring the boy to me." And then Jesus healed the son, not despite of but *because* of this man's not-enough and just-enough faith. When I was done, the church voted to hire me, a young and inexperienced person, as their lead pastor—taking, I now see, their own leap of faith.

But I wasn't done with that prayer. I wasn't done with needing to bring Roxanne to Jesus. I would have to bring her a few short days later, the day after my graduation from seminary, when we got the surgery results. The cancer was in the lymph nodes. It was at least stage three. She would need intensive cancer treatment. The outcomes looked very bleak.

I would have to bring her again and again as I started a new job amid a season of fear. I had to bring her when I googled "prognosis stage three melanoma," while the musicians practiced before church one Sunday, and read *10 percent survival past five years.* ("Why would you google that on a Sunday morning?" my husband asked, gently, when he found me sobbing twenty minutes before the service started.)

I would pray incessantly when my fears and worries crowded out any sense of peace I tried to hold. *I do believe, God. Help me overcome my unbelief.* I would learn to trust that my faith wasn't doing the work but God was. *Bring her to me.*

Doubt-filled faith is the norm for a whole lot of people. As I settled into my role as pastor, I soon saw how many needed this same space for an uncertain faith.

Len and Dorothy, a couple in their early eighties, were absolutely devastated when Len was diagnosed with cancer. "Oh, Leanne," Dorothy said, sitting on her plush couch with framed pictures of her children and grandchildren on a shelf behind them. "I know it isn't the worst thing to ever happen, but it's the worst thing to ever happen *to us.*" And then she confessed what she had been embarrassed to say: she was frightened. She had been a Christian her entire life—a faith that spanned decades—and now she wasn't sure what to do next.

I didn't tell her she had to "just trust God" or that she needed to "have more faith." I reminded her of the story of a father who wanted his little boy healed and jumbled over his words to Jesus: "I do believe. Help my unbelief." Dorothy wept with relief and thanked me. "I have felt like it's all my fault for being so scared," she said.

I remember Betty too. Betty got cancer in her eye in her late seventies, and she was angry. She'd never been very involved in the church, and I'm still not sure what she believed about God, but she did have an idea that she deserved something better. She was a good person; why couldn't criminals be the ones to get cancer instead of her?

But she was also scared. Betty wanted to be honest about how frightened she was, and it infuriated her that every time she told someone she was afraid, they would tell her she shouldn't be. "Think positive!" they would say.

So I told Betty about a dad who said to Jesus: "I do believe. Help me overcome my unbelief." In fact, I ended up telling her that story often because each time I visited, she would ask me to remind her. To her, this was real hope. There was room for her to be scared and uncertain. Two years later, I told the story at her funeral.

Eight years after I preached on that passage as a trial sermon, almost to the week, I would preach on that same text again. It would be my first sermon back in the pulpit after Roxanne died. And I would realize that I knew even less about faith than I thought I did when I preached on this passage the first time as a prospective pastor. And I would realize that was okay.

Faith isn't a work that we do; it is a gift that God gives. My faith hadn't healed Roxanne, but God had granted me enough faith to keep returning to God day after day, year after year, surgery after surgery. God gave me this faith not despite my fears but in the middle of them—not because I was certain I could have enough faith but because I knew I couldn't.

Our uncertainty needs room. We need room to be disappointed when prayers for healing aren't answered. We need room to not always be sure what we believe. We need room to be like a father who says, "I do believe. Help me overcome my unbelief," without fear that we're blowing it in the faith department.

Even if we don't believe in God, we can all feel pressure when facing hard things to "have a little faith" that things will turn out all right. It can be hard when we feel like we can't "think positive" enough or "just believe" enough to ensure the right outcome. It's a lot of pressure to connect a certain attitude to a healing outcome, and I don't believe we need to.

In uncertain times, perfect faith or cheerful optimism is not always what we need most. Sometimes we need room for a little uncertainty. We need space to take one shaky step at a time.

2

ROOM FOR THE "AND"
MAKING SPACE FOR ALL THE DAYS IN THE CALENDAR

Calendars can be complicated.

Sometimes the pages of an untouched calendar seem hopeful and exciting. We see a year ahead of us, full of promise and possibility. Turning a calendar to a new day, or a new month, or a new year can feel like a fresh start, with the blank pages before us free to make anything we want. But a calendar can be frightening if we know that difficult things are likely. When we are sick, grieving, or preparing for death, a calendar can be a haunting reminder of the limited days of our lives, the many days to come without our loved one with us, or simply a terrifying cosmic countdown.

For many years, I had a Christmas calendar gift tradition with my nieces and nephews. I purchased each of them a "page-a-day" desktop calendar, the kind where you tear off one sheet each new day. They've always got some sort of a theme, like a picture of a puppy or a funny joke on every page. To personalize these gifts for my nieces and nephews, I would add little notes throughout the year on every third or fourth page, as a way to connect with them from a distance. I'd include little messages about things I loved about them, or my favorite memories with them, or goofy trivia I thought they would find funny.

I loved this tradition very much until the year I felt very differently about calendars: the fall when I held the calendars for the year that I knew Roxanne would die.

After Roxanne's diagnosis and first surgery, cancer became a regular part of our lives for the next eight years. Roxanne completed her first surgery and then a year of treatments, only to discover one week before the treatment was finished that she had a new growth on her back and would have to start the whole cycle again. She had another aggressive surgery, more treatment to face. Her cancer was relentless.

For nearly a decade, she had to constantly get new growths checked and removed. She gathered scars and was left with whole chunks of her body missing as the doctors dug deep to remove the new melanomas each time they appeared. She let her hair grow long for the first time in years to cover the noticeable indent on her neck. She stopped wearing shirts with low backs to cover the giant depression on her back. She was always checking, always monitoring, always fighting cancer in some way or another.

When you or someone you love is sick with a long-term or life-threatening illness, one of the tricky things is learning how to even explain it to people. Everyone wants a clear answer, a prognosis, a gauge of how worried they should or should not be. We learned how to explain to people how melanoma worked: that it could function like a chronic disease. "Picture someone throwing balls at you, one after the other," we would say to confused relatives or friends seeking clarity about Roxanne's health when they heard about another growth and assumed the worst. "At first, you can catch them one at a time. But if the balls keep getting faster and faster, you stop being able to catch them." For eight years, Roxanne was constantly trying to keep up with the balls thrown at her, but she also knew that one day they would come too fast. Every possible future event in her life—from her children's graduations to a summer vacation—was tempered with the fear that she might not be here.

Despite her best effort at catching those balls, she eventually moved from stage three melanoma to stage four. There was another treatment, another surgery, and more suffering. After her last aggressive round of radiation, she had to live with the knowledge that her body would never be able to have radiation safely again. Should the cancer spread, no more remedies that her body would tolerate remained. If the balls started to fly again, there were no proven ways left to catch them.

A lot happened in those eight years. Roxanne attended her children's piano recitals, volleyball tournaments, and orchestra practices. She led the children's Christmas pageant at her church each year and invited more and more people to her annual New Year's Eve party every December 31. She kept teaching, a job that she loved, and her amazing coworkers threw her a big party on the day she passed her five-year survival mark. Roxanne and her family flew helicopters over volcanoes in Hawaii, cruised along the coast of California, and swam with turtles in the warm water of Costa Rica. There were so many wonderful things—but there was always cancer. Always surgeries. Always new growths. Always fear.

We knew the statistics, that the five-year survival for people with Roxanne's type of cancer was less than 10 percent. By 2013 we would be heading into year eight. We had been catching the balls a long time. Still, we tried to be optimistic. Maybe, *maybe,* she could keep being the miracle she already was. Maybe she would be the anomaly. Maybe she would beat every odd!

Then the leg growth came. You couldn't actually see anything, but Roxanne could feel a little nodule lodged firmly in her upper right thigh, and she knew. The tests came back: definitely a melanoma, definitely spreading. I remember receiving the call in my office on a warm day in June 2012. I stayed calm on the phone, told Roxanne I loved her, reminded her that we were all in this together. But I knew she was hearing the same voice echoing around her head that I was, the one that said, "No more treatments. No more treatments."

Those calls are hard ones when we know what they can mean for the days of the calendar before us. Many of us have heard our own echoed fears: "No treatments." "Last attempts." "Prepare for the worst." We want to freeze time, will the pages on the way to stop turning. But we can't. It can be terrifying to know that our worst days are ahead of us, with no way to stop them and no way to predict when they will fall.

There was the first of a few experimental options. A long shot. We knew it was never meant to be curative. Like many with cancer before her, Roxanne followed a game plan to buy some proverbial time, with the hope that a more permanent treatment option might become available in the meantime. She had an MRI scheduled for October, which would show if the experimental option had made any difference. I ended up being home in Newfoundland on the day she got the results from the test.

We sat in the packed cancer clinic waiting room before her appointment, waiting for Mike to join us. As we chatted, Roxanne commented that it looked like I had lost some weight. I had been working out and eating better, but I commented that I wasn't sure if I'd lost weight since we didn't have a scale at home.

"Well, let's weigh you now. There's a scale right there!" she said, pointing to a device in front of us in the crowded waiting room.

"I don't think I should," I said, glancing over my shoulder at the people around us. I mean, was it really okay to weigh myself at a *cancer clinic?*

"Oh, come on," she said. "No one knows why you're here!"

So I quickly got on the scale and read the numbers. It said I had not lost weight. "Well, that can't be right," Roxanne frowned. "You have *clearly* lost weight. It shows!" This was classic Roxanne, wanting everyone to succeed. She would rather say an expensive medical instrument was broken than suggest that I hadn't achieved something I wanted.

"We need to find a different one . . . Come on!" And she pulled me into a hall.

This area of the ward was obviously meant to be more private, but there was, indeed, a scale at the end of the hall. Roxanne dragged me to it. "Use this one!" she commanded. Now I felt even more uncertain. The other scale was public, and people were getting on and off it all the time. I could blend in with the crowd. Now it really seemed like we were somewhere we weren't quite supposed to be. I hesitated.

"Who's going to see you? There's no one here!" Roxanne pointed out.

"Oh, all right," I answered, and just as I put one foot on the machine, we heard an exuberant voice echo down the hall: "ROXANNE AND LEANNE!"

The two of us screamed. I jumped back to the floor so quickly that the scale started to shake. It was an old neighbor of ours who now worked at the cancer clinic. She was calling out to say hello, but we were so startled that we reacted as if we had been caught committing a crime.

And then we laughed. We *roared* with laughter. We laughed until we couldn't breathe. Soon the only sound in the hall was the wheeze of us trying to catch our breath. Our friend stared at us, dumbfounded. We tried to explain to her what was so funny, but we just seemed to confuse her.

Eventually she gave up and mumbled that she had to get back to work. We were still giggling as we waved goodbye. We went back to the waiting room, tears still streaming down our faces. When Mike showed up, we tried to explain to him why we were in hysterics in the cancer clinic, but we couldn't even get the words out. When we were called into the doctor's office, we were still recovering, chuckling under our breath as we thought of the terror we felt when we heard our names, as if we had been caught robbing a bank instead of standing on a scale in an empty hall.

It was time for Roxanne to disrobe, so the doctor could see the "leg growth." I hadn't seen it since the summer, when I still had to push my finger on her leg to feel it. When she lifted the corner of her paper robe to show me her leg, I gasped. The melanoma had grown to the size of my fist, and it was pronounced, pink, and terrifying. My reaction was not subtle. "I guess it looks pretty bad, huh?" Roxanne asked me.

I apologized. "Kind of failed on the non-anxious presence there," I told her, "Not so good for a pastor that's supposed to be good at this. Let me try again."

I cleared my throat and, in a deadpan voice, said, "That is a really interesting goiter you have growing out of your leg, Roxanne." She grinned as I continued. "I see that it is the size of my fist. It looks rather terrible. Please note I have no emotions about this." Now Roxanne was full belly laughing.

I was still doing my deadpan "non-anxious" voice describing her horrible tumor when the doctor came in. After seven years of treatments, he knew her well. This was the moment when we would hear "life" or "death." The doctor took a stool and rolled it over. He sat down on it and looked Roxanne in the eyes. And he sighed.

It was the sigh that told us everything.

We stopped laughing.

Why had none of us thought to bring a notepad? I'll still never know. But I had a scrap of paper in my purse, and I scratched down each piece of information I could fit. Fragments of life-changing words next to a grocery list:

Spread.
Spots in the neck, arm, lungs.
Cancer in the liver.

Roxanne asked for a sick note for work for a few days, and the doctor replied, "Oh, Roxanne, why don't you just stop working now?" This was it, then. We couldn't catch the balls anymore. It was all stunning, really. Even though we had been preparing for seven years.

As we left the hospital, I told Roxanne I would call our parents. I would give them the news that their daughter was dying, so she wouldn't have to.

I tried to explain it that day on the phone to my parents. Day after day, I would explain it again. But they never seemed to quite process it. Their questions never made sense. They still asked about things like treatment and surgery. Gently, consistently, I told them this was all there was. This was it. This was the news.

A few days later, I was at Roxanne's house. We were watching TV, and during a commercial, she said, out of nowhere, "I wish I could have gone to the girls' graduation."

I said, "Me too."

We kept watching.

And in my suitcase, I had two unopened page-a-day calendars to give to Emily and Hannah for Christmas. I had packed them, figuring I could write the messages during my trip and then leave the calendars at their house, thus saving on the cost of postage. Now the calendars mocked me. Each day, I saw them, sitting in my bag. I didn't know how to face them. This, I realized, was the year that Roxanne would die. This was the year Emily and Hannah's mother would die. How was I supposed to write notes in these calendars?

What if, on the day Roxanne ended up dying, I wrote something truly stupid, like "Did you know nothing rhymes with orange?" What days should include a message, and what days should I skip? Should I still write, "Happy Birthday to your mom!" on her birthday in February? Would she still be here? Would I write, "Happy Anniversary to your parents!" in December, still over a year away at that point?

It was too much. It was too soon. Looking to the start of the year and knowing what would come overwhelmed me each time I even considered the calendars. The presents sat in my suitcase, taunting me. I hated those stupid calendars, hated the year they held within their pages.

I'm not the first person to face a new year with dread because of what I know will happen in it. Sometimes new calendars are not our friends. No picture of a kitten or quote from our favorite movie on a calendar's page can hide the sinister reality that the time before us holds. Nothing I could write for my nieces would stop the inevitable that was on the way in 2013. Nothing we do will stop the pages turning.

Some time later, I was asked to speak on Lamentations 3 at a women's conference. The theme verse was Lamentations 3:23: "Because of the Lord's great love we are not consumed." That verse comes at the most unexpected place in the Bible. The entirety of Lamentations 3 is a passage of sorrow—more accurately, in my opinion, *outrage*.

The whole book, scholars believe, was written during a time after Jerusalem had been invaded and sacked by the Babylonians in 597 BCE. Many of the former residents of the city had been taken into exile, as it was the tactic of the Babylonians at the time to take the "brightest and best" with them to their capital. They'd leave behind defeated cities, and those who lived in them, in ruin.

Lamentations was written by someone still in the city of Jerusalem after this tragedy. The remaining residents are broken and despondent, and in Lamentations 3, they make no bones about it. They say that they are afflicted, that their flesh has wasted away, that they call to God and are met with only silence.

Then, out of what seems to be nowhere, appears this verse: "Because of the Lord's great love we are not consumed. . . . The Lord's mercies are new every morning." This is one of my favorite passages in the Bible because it is an *and* message. An *and* message acknowledges the dialectic of faith: that two things can be true at the same time. Like the father with the sick son, I believe, *and* I need help to believe. Or in this case: Everything around the author is falling apart, *and* they will not be consumed.

I love *and* messages because we need them in a life where we find ourselves often defaulting to using the word *but*. I am hopeful, *but* I'm afraid. I'm doing my best, *but* I'm worried. I trust the best will happen, *but* I'm really struggling.

Saying "but" in this passage from Lamentations would have made a lot of sense. "We believe in God, but our city is destroyed." "God is supposed to be good? But look what happened!" I know that if I was looking at my ruined city—remembering the thousands who had died and noticing all those taken into captivity—I would be screaming out that God was unfair, that there was no way for there to be good here. "But *look* at what happened to us!" I would holler.

And that's what I wanted to yell when I looked at those calendars. "Yeah, I always do these calendars for my nieces, *but look—their mother is going to die this year!*"

The idea of losing my sister, of facing the year of her death, shook all my foundations. How could I celebrate a year that would likely be the one in which her life ended? How could I fill in those calendars?

The answer, I realized after a few days, was found in that verse: "Because of the Lord's great love, we are not consumed." The answer for me was this: God would still, somehow, be in every day of that calendar. My sister was going to die. She was going to die in 2013. *And* I would not be consumed.

It occurred to me that of all the years that my nieces might need messages from their aunt to remind them they were loved, the coming year might be the year they needed them most. So one evening toward the end of my stay with them, I slowly cracked the calendars' pages and started to write, trusting that God would guide my hands and my words so that I could write what was needed on the right day. I could be sad that a terrible year was coming—*and* I could fill in the calendars.

It was not unlike my day at the cancer clinic with Roxanne. That appointment with her doctor was one of the hardest moments of my life—*and* the moment we stood on those scales and shrieked at the sound of our names is one of my very favorite memories with Roxanne. An awful moment *and* a cherished memory, all within the same hour. Humor and horror on the same day. Laughing and wailing, all together.

I finished the calendars, little by little. I wished Roxanne happy birthday in February, but I left their wedding anniversary blank. It was the right choice. On Roxanne's birthday, she was still with us and still well. By December, she had already been dead for seven months.

On May 4, 2013, the day she died, I crawled back home to Roxanne's house after leaving the hospital. Before I got into bed, I took a peek at the calendars on the girls' nightstands where they kept them. I looked at May 4, holding my breath, hoping that I hadn't written something silly.

On that day, I had written nothing. And I took a deep breath and said a prayer of thanks to God.

As we face the hardest things in our lives, we need room for the *and*. I could be scared of 2013 *and* I could face it. I could hate 2013 *and* I could survive it. My sister was going to die in 2013 *and* I could fill in calendars.

We all need room for the *and* when we face grief and loss. We need room for tears and room for giggles. We need room for bad days and room for days that aren't so bad. We need room for frustration at injustice and room for gratitude at what is good. Sometimes that room will look like being relieved that our person is no longer suffering one minute and pleading with God to give them back the next. Sometimes it will look like talking about how absolutely wonderful they were and admitting they sometimes drove you crazy at the same time. Making room for *and* can mean declaring that something is impossible and doing it anyway. "I can't clean out their clothes from my house." "I can't speak at the funeral." "I can't make this decision." *And* then, somehow, you do. Making room for *and* includes letting a whole bunch of feelings exist at the same time. It means that you can be as hurt, despairing, hopeful, and optimistic as you find you are. It means not having to pick one feeling over another, no matter what the days of the calendar will bring.

You might not have answers or certainty. You might have anger and outrage. You might feel overwhelmed, indignant, cheated, or resigned. That's okay. Sometimes things simply *can't* be okay. And we keep going, one day of the calendar at a time.

3

ROOM FOR THE GRIEF TO COME
PLEASE LET ME SAY MY LOVED ONE IS DYING

The winter came, and Roxanne made it through Christmas. Some days I thought, "Maybe the cancer wasn't growing!" Maybe we had misunderstood what the doctor had said, as my parents, my brother, and my other sister suggested all the time. But deep down, I knew I hadn't. I had heard him sigh.

Still, even though I knew these things, I was also thankful for how healthy Roxanne still was. Besides the ever-growing mound on her leg, Roxanne didn't seem to be getting any sicker. We put our worries on pause over Christmas. But I got another call at my office in January, after Roxanne's latest checkup. Roxanne's voice was hollow. "The doctor said weeks, maybe months."

I mean, sometimes we know the truth even when we don't think we know it.

The night of that phone call, I attended a rally to protest the building of a casino in our city's downtown. While I was there, I saw a close friend. I told him about the news we had heard that day, and he asked, "Why are you *here* tonight?"

I paused. Why had I come? Why wasn't I at home, in a ball, crying? Why was I surrounding myself with people and protests when I had my own terrible thing to deal with?

I knew the answer: "Because I don't want to live in a world where my sister is dead *and* there's also a casino in the poorest part of my city."

He nodded. "That makes sense," he said. There are different kinds of darkness, and we stand up to the ones we can.

We wanted to spend more time together. I planned a trip home for a long weekend in February. Our other sister, Deanne, decided to come, too, and then Jason decided to drive across Newfoundland to be with us. A siblings' weekend!

Roxanne had some worries about this enterprise. "It's not going to be some morbid weekend about me dying, is it?" I promised her it wouldn't, not sure if this was a realistic commitment. Could we walk the emotional tightrope we were about to navigate? Could we gather for what was almost certainly a final weekend together with Roxanne still healthy without thinking about Roxanne's death all the time? We would have to try. But soon I would see the reality of what the next few months would look like for all of us: the constant tension of embracing life as death was creeping in, the grief that was already nudging its way into our lives.

The balancing act began as soon as we all got to St. John's. We went shopping. I had vowed to not buy anything on this trip. I had intentionally only brought a small carry-on, so I wouldn't be tempted. But this was always futile with Roxanne. We went to a funky consignment store, and Roxanne kept getting me to try things on. I tried on a wrap dress, which I loved. "You have to buy it!" Roxanne said, "It suits you!" As usual when we shopped together, Roxanne prevailed. I squeezed the dress into my tiny suitcase, along with the blouse Roxanne had talked me into buying. And of course, there were the gifts she had purchased for my kids, and the books she insisted on sending them, and her girls' toys she wanted to pass on. As she watched me pack to leave, I laughed. "Why did I even bother only packing a carry-on?" I asked. She acknowledged it had been a bad idea.

We went to the mall, where she found a fabulous suede blazer—on sale! "You should definitely get it!" I said. She waffled, as she always did when deciding to buy something; only this time she added, "Leanne, I might never get to wear it." This was true. She was still working and feeling well, but she was starting one more Hail Mary treatment her doctor had rummaged up in a couple of days. Would she really need a blazer?

"Well," I said, "It's such a good price that even if you wear it once, it's a good deal." This was a favorite shopping argument of Roxanne's.

"You're right!" she perked up, walking to the checkout. "It *is* a good deal."

We were buying a blazer, and death was creeping in. What *if* she never got to wear it?

Roxanne said that she had booked photos for the four of us. I had wanted to suggest this same idea but had worried that taking last photos together might fall in the category of "sad and morbid weekend." But Roxanne said she wanted to be sure she had a good headshot for her obituary. We agreed that this made sense.

It wasn't a fancy photo shoot. We went to the local grocery store, which did those "seven thousand pictures for twenty dollars" kind of deals. The photographer was a teenager who would take a shot and let us look to decide if we liked it before she continued. We got pictures of the four of us, huddled together, laughing, and then each of us with Roxanne as a pair. Then Roxanne sat for her photo by herself, and we tried to get her to smile just right, prompting her to turn her head just so, to cover the gap in her teeth on the left side while highlighting her dimple at the same time.

"Does anyone else want a headshot?" the photographer asked when Roxanne was done.

"No thanks," we answered. The poor young photographer looked confused. "So just you for a shot by yourself?" she asked Roxanne. We nodded.

In the car on the way home, we laughed about it. "Should we have said you were getting ready for your obituary?" we asked Roxanne. Somehow the idea struck us as funny, and we joked about it all the way home. We were experiencing another *and*: hilarious and horrendous, all rolled together. We often laughed as we coped with doing things too painful to analyze closely.

Packing my photos carefully in the bottom of my suitcase, taped between cardboard to keep them safe, with the new clothes and gifts on top, I tried not to think of the relics the things in my suitcase were quickly becoming. The last blouse bought with Roxanne. The last photo. The last gift. The suitcase really wasn't big enough for the memories and the heartbreak, all crammed in there together.

We decided to buy some hats.

The treatment that would start on the Tuesday after we left had a slim chance of working—a 2 percent chance of giving Roxanne a couple of more months. And it would come with side effects. For the first time since having cancer, Roxanne would lose her hair.

Off we went to a hat store downtown, determined to find some hats, wigs, and scarves for when the inevitable happened. The salesperson, who quickly learned why we were there, was used to having cancer patients in her store. She joined in our shopping and gave lots of great practical advice. She discouraged Roxanne from spending a lot on a wig. She explained that most of the people she knew ended up wearing simple scarves or nothing at all; the wigs were just too uncomfortable. She directed her to some beautiful loose headscarves that we raved about. She took pictures of us wearing matching wigs. We were genuinely having a great time. We were enjoying shopping and pretending it had nothing to do with cancer.

There was only one source of awkwardness. The clerk kept making comments about when Roxanne's hair grew back, discussing in passing what it would be like when she "got better." She kept showing Roxanne options of what to wear for her transition back to her "normal hair." Roxanne looked at me with a sad smile. Who wanted to break it to the salesperson that there would not be time for Roxanne's hair to grow back before cancer took over?

Finally, I made eye contact with the clerk. Roxanne was distracted at the moment, and as I met eyes with the kind woman, who was holding out another "transition wig," I closed my eyes and made the slightest shake of my head. She stumbled on a sentence for a second, then recovered her composure. She put the wig aside and discreetly moved to another area. She didn't mention Roxanne's hair growing back again. She understood the tightrope we were on.

Roxanne's daughters were slated to sing the song "Come to Jesus" in their church that Sunday. Mike had prepared a slideshow to go with it. The song goes through different phases of life and invites people to "come to Jesus" in those moments. The last verse ends by assuring the listener not to be afraid to die but to "come to Jesus" in peace when their life ends.

We all loved listening to Emily and Hannah practice this song over the weekend. But it was also hard to keep the emotions in check as we heard the girls sing that last verse, hard not to think of that prayer as one for Roxanne. We knew other people in the congregation would think the same. At one point I said, "Roxanne, you know that song is going to set everyone off, right?"

"What do you mean?" she asked.

"I mean the whole church will be sobbing when your girls sing about going to be with Jesus," I said.

"Really?" Roxanne asked, genuinely surprised. "You think people will cry?"

"Um, yes, Roxanne," I said, as the rest of our siblings started to laugh. "I definitely think your girls singing about heaven might just make people cry."

She laughed, too, realizing what was about to happen, but also with a little heaviness. I realized that it was time to keep my end of our "don't make this weekend morbid" bargain.

"Now," I said. "If we really want to be sure people cry, we should dress you up like an angel—we all know we can make that happen with all the costumes you've collected in the basement. And then on the last verse, we put up a picture of you in the angel costume looking like this." I posed, looking solemn, one leg in the air behind me, hands in a Superman position. "You know, like you're flying to heaven."

I suggested other poses, and Roxanne and my siblings were laughing hard at the lunacy of it all. I had gone a little far with my joke, but it had worked. Yes, Roxanne agreed, when she could stop laughing, if we stuck a picture of her as a flying angel at the end of the slideshow, it might just cause a reaction.

The last day we were all together, Roxanne started to feel sick. "I think I have a bladder infection," she suggested. In our makeshift bedroom in their rec room later, Deanne looked at me. "It's not a bladder infection, is it?"

"No," I answered. We took deep breaths. We went back to Roxanne. We smiled, played another game.

We all knew it wasn't a bladder infection.

I stayed one day longer than anyone else, one day with just me and Roxanne. We went out for lunch, and we ordered sandwiches and salads with fries to share. After a few lighthearted minutes of chatting, the conversation turned. Roxanne began explaining the likelihood the treatment wouldn't work. She wanted to prepare me, I think. Did I understand that this only had a slim chance of making any difference? Did I understand that even if it did, we were only talking about her surviving a few extra weeks?

"This could be our last lunch out," she told me.

As much as Roxanne wanted to, even she couldn't keep her death away that weekend. It was there always, creeping its way in. We didn't know it for sure, but we would never eat lunch together again. We were sharing our own last supper.

And then I was back in Ontario, far from Roxanne. But her looming death was everywhere, a shadow lurking in every corner of my life. An elderly man at our church died, and I officiated at his funeral. As I stood at his grave on a freezing February day and watched his casket being carried to his grave, it hit me like a wave: soon the person in the casket would be Roxanne.

A woman's brother died. His daughter asked if I would go to tell her aunt in person since she knew she would need someone with her when she heard the news. I went to her aunt's workplace and asked to see her. When she came and saw me waiting in her boss's office, she knew. She collapsed into my arms as she cried, "My baby brother is gone."

What would I do when I heard Roxanne was dead, I wondered. Where would I collapse? Who would catch me?

The father of a congregant died. When I went to the hospital to be with the family, I watched. I looked on as they said their goodbyes to the body of the man they loved, lying in a hospital bed. I watched them when the time came to leave the hospital. I always wondered how people did that—how they walked away for the last time. I wondered how we would know when to leave the room when only Roxanne's body remained.

For a few weeks, Roxanne did the treatment, and then she went to find out if it had made any difference. It was a Monday when I got another call at the office, the last office call I would ever receive from Roxanne.

"Well, it didn't work," Roxanne told me. The cancer was everywhere. This was really—*really*—it.

"I'm so sorry," I told her.

"Well, there it is," she answered. She went on to explain that she and Mike had stopped at the funeral home after her appointment and made her arrangements. And then we talked about her funeral.

This wasn't actually a new thing. Since having cancer, Roxanne had often discussed her funeral with me. She would mention it to me in passing, tell me details that mattered to her. I think this may have been because I was a minister, and she knew me to be comfortable talking about funerals, and also because she knew I would remember her requests.

Now she said something I had anticipated for a long time. "I want you to do my eulogy—and I want it to be *fun.*"

She had told me this before. For the years during which we knew she had cancer, I had thought of how I would eulogize her. I had always hoped, of course, I would never actually need to do it. I responded, with tears she couldn't see streaming down my face, "Absolutely, Roxanne, and I promise I'll *show right off!*"

Roxanne started laughing. This was an old joke in our family, something my mom always said. Having grown up poor in rural Newfoundland, Mom had always drilled into us that we should always be proud to show what we could do. She loved to encourage us to "show off" to anyone we could—in particular, townies (slang for those who lived in the city of St. John's) and mainlanders (those who live outside of Newfoundland). When we would do things in public, this was often her mantra. "Show right off!" she would tell us, as we got up to perform at a speech contest or play at a music recital. What it meant was, "Don't hold back. Give it everything you've got. Show them what you can do."

I opened a file on my computer, called it "Roxanne's Eulogy," and saw it every time I logged on for the next month under my "recent documents." Roxanne's death was everywhere, even in my file folder.

Then Good Friday came, a day when Christians remember the death of Jesus. That year, I knew there was one thing I wanted to do. I asked a woman from our church if she would sing a song with me—"Abide with Me," a song often reserved for funerals, which talks about God being with us in the last days of life. That Good Friday, I felt every word of that song. It was only on the last line that my voice caught a little: "In life, in death, Oh Lord, abide with me."

I still remember looking out and seeing a man from our church with tears in his eyes. As we sang that simple line, he did something he probably didn't realize he was doing—he nodded. I knew much of this man's story. I knew that his mother had died suddenly some years before, and I knew that he had grieved that loss ever since. Of all the things I remember from that season, that nod is one of them: that simple nod that said, "Yes, Christ is with us in death." That nod that saw the sorrow hovering around my life.

I wore the wrap dress that I'd bought with Roxanne at the consignment shop as I sang. Roxanne lay in bed one thousand miles away, the beige blazer hanging in her closet that would never be worn again.

The day after Easter, I flew back to Newfoundland again. There were no mall runs, no lunches out, no games, no sing-alongs. This time there was just Roxanne in her bed, dying one day at a time. Death, everywhere, and so much else.

There were so many *people*. How could one person know so many people? But she did. Roxanne collected friends in every part of her life, and it seemed that everyone wanted to visit that week. The house was always full of coworkers, neighbors, old high school friends, cousins, aunts, uncles, and in-laws.

I didn't always know where I fit. Was it selfish to want Roxanne to myself? Of course everyone wanted time alone with her. Everyone wanted to have "one final conversation," one "moment of goodbye." I soon saw how exhausting this was for Roxanne. Day after day, people would come and cry over her bedside, saying how much they loved her. Roxanne never shed a tear. She was too busy with her dying to look after others.

I remember Roxanne's response after one neighbor had sobbed on her shoulder, wailing, "You've been the best neighbor we could ask for!" The woman shuffled out, wiping her tears, and Roxanne looked at me and said softly, "I can't keep doing this." What was one conversation for everyone else was adding up to unending conversations for her, and it was too much. I was determined not to be another person that Roxanne felt she had to look after. I would be a safe space. I would keep my feelings in check. My only goal was to care for Roxanne. I would demand nothing of her.

For ten days, I did very little. I read while she slept. I talked to visitors so they wouldn't overwhelm Roxanne. I lay next to her on her bed as we watched *American Idol* episodes. One day she said, "I can't believe I'm not going to find out who wins."

Roxanne snuggled a little closer as we kept watching.

Sometimes I was jealous. She had a friend who had flown in from Alberta just to visit her. Three days in a row, Wanda came to visit, and we would all vacate the room so Roxanne could have time with her. By day three, I was feeling annoyed. I adored Wanda, but why did she get so much *time*? What about *me*? I was her *sister*, for pity's sake, and I had flown from far away too!

Sometimes I was jealous of Mike, who got to sleep next to her every night, whose role was so obvious and clear. I was jealous of her best friend, Darlene, who had been there for weeks already and so easily stepped into the role as caregiver. I wanted that role, even as I knew I would have to leave it again when I returned to Ontario.

But there were always so many people, so many times that I felt like just another person in the crowd, so many moments that I wanted more than I could get and more than I could ask Roxanne to give. I felt her death every minute, and all I could think was, "Will I have any good time with her again? Is this it?"

Roxanne asked me if I would go through her pictures to help get her slideshow ready for her funeral. She wanted to vet every photograph that would go in the slideshow. I spent hours poring over Roxanne's perfectly labeled photo albums. Pictures of teenage Roxanne on her first trip to Scotland. Roxanne covered in mud when she bathed in the

Dead Sea. Roxanne and Mike sitting on a green hillside in Ireland. Roxanne and her friends dancing and singing at a party, dressed for a skit at family camp, enjoying a vacation. Baby Roxanne with my parents, New Mom Roxanne with her children. So many pictures of me as a baby, with thirteen-year-old Roxanne holding me proudly.

I would go through an album or two, select pictures I thought would work, and bring them up for Roxanne's approval. The Dead Sea picture in a swimsuit was rejected. Every picture with her children got a nod. I spent hours picking photos, making sure no segment of her life or people who mattered to her would be forgotten.

There was so much food: people offering food, people dropping off food, people asking what food we liked. There were meals every night, snacks every minute, and an inexplicable and unending supply of muffins. I don't know how or why it happened, but at one point we counted over a hundred muffins on the kitchen counter. We started to freeze extras, send them home with family members. I dubbed the counter "Muffin Mountain."

Roxanne was eating little, but one day I suggested I could get her a smoothie. She thought she could try one. I went to a local smoothie place and ordered the exact smoothie I had liked when I was pregnant and struggling with severe nausea. I brought it home, and Roxanne drank the whole thing. The next day, she asked for another one.

Somehow word got out that Roxanne was drinking smoothies. Now everyone showed up with smoothies for her, of every variety. We collected the Smoothie Cups next to Muffin Mountain. But Roxanne didn't drink any of them. Roxanne liked the kind that I had got her, the very simple blend that I knew was good for nausea. She only ever drank my concoctions, and I held on to the one thing I had to offer. I couldn't do much, but I could get her the right smoothies.

She drank smoothies, and we ate muffins.

"What should I wear in my casket?" she asked me one day.

"Do you want to pick something out?" I asked her. She did. I began to hold up outfits from her closet. "Too black," she said to some. "I don't like that one," she said about another. I kept pulling out outfits. At one point, I pulled out a flowery blouse I hadn't seen her wear before.

"Wait! Try that on! You should take that one home!" She explained that it had been a birthday gift, and she had never even worn it. Plus, it was a size too big for her, so she was certain it would fit me. I humored her and tried it on. "Yes," she smiled delightedly, "You have to take that with you! It looks great on you." She was dying in her bed, and she was still giving me clothes.

I put it aside, ready to pack for later. By now, Roxanne had grown tired. Exhausted, she decided to let Darlene decide what she would wear when the time came. Roxanne was already letting things go.

The days were weird, busy, empty. Full of nothing. Full of too much. Muffins. *American Idol.* Staying out of the way. Trying to stay close. I read *Jane Eyre.* I played online Scrabble. I felt my heart break into pieces.

And then one day, Roxanne and I were alone. It seemed impossible. We were never alone. It was early in the morning. Darlene hadn't come yet. My parents hadn't come yet. Mike had gone outside to shovel snow. The girls were at school. Roxanne had gotten out of bed and was sitting in her living room, something she had only managed a couple of times the whole month.

I felt it everywhere, her death. I felt the reality that this could be the last conversation I might have with a lucid Roxanne. I couldn't help myself. I had to say something.

So for the first time, I told her about my dream. I told her about the dream I had eight years earlier, before I knew she had cancer: the dream in which she died, in which music about God's will had been playing. I had convinced myself that sharing this with her might bring her comfort.

She just nodded. And paused. And then she said quietly, "I don't know why I didn't get healed."

There it was. The thing none of us understood. The truth was I didn't know either. I had no idea why someone so wonderful, so kind, so supportive of others didn't get to have a few more years on this earth. I had spent a week watching hundreds of people pour through her house, saying what a difference Roxanne made in their lives. Nothing about her death made sense. There was no way to justify it.

"I don't know either," I said.

It was quiet for a moment, and I suddenly found myself blurting out, "I wish we could have been old ladies together."

Roxanne smiled. "We could have gone to Florida," she said.

Something inside of me shattered. Suddenly I could picture that Florida trip vividly in my mind. I could picture us at the outlet stores, going for lunch every day, putting our feet in the warm sand. I could picture the fun we would have had as old ladies, bustling around together and complaining about the humidity.

"I would've liked that," I said. Then Mike came back inside, and that was that.

My last night, I crawled into bed with her. She had been asleep, but I needed to talk to her one more time. My vow of not disturbing her was broken, once again. I couldn't resist, couldn't leave without hearing her voice again, without trying to have a moment of meaning.

As I snuggled next to her in her bed one last time, she woke briefly. "I dreamed I was swimming with turtles," she said.

"I'm leaving tomorrow," I told her. "I love you."

"I love you too," she mumbled, her voice still full of sleep.

"You have been a wonderful sister."

"You've been a wonderful sister too."

She fell back asleep, and I crawled out of bed, packed my suitcase, and got ready for my early morning flight.

And one day a short time later, I was at my church, and someone asked me how Roxanne was doing. And I said, "Well, she's dying," and she said, "Don't say that!"

Perhaps now you can see exactly how bizarre this comment seemed to me. I was surrounded by my sister dying. I was picking out funeral slideshow photos. I was discussing what she should wear in her casket. I was writing her eulogy.

Not say she was dying? What else did I have to say? Her dying was my story every day, every minute, every second. I needed room for her coming death. I wasn't yet grieving, but I was already grieving. And I needed room for that grief.

It still baffles me when I look back to remember how hard it was to find the room I needed at that time. Funny enough, it was my six-year-old son who seemed to get it most. One night as I lay in bed after a long day, my husband came in our room and told me what Josiah had asked to pray for during his bedtime prayers. "Leanne," he said, "Josiah asked if we could pray for Aunt Roxanne on her trip to heaven."

I fell apart. I got up, went back to my living room, sat staring out the window, even though I was blinded by my overflowing tears. Dallas sat beside me, saying nothing. The perfect words had already been said. Roxanne was getting ready for her trip to heaven, and we needed to pray for her. My sweet boy had gotten it just right. I have thought often of how my six-year-old seemed to have wisdom that surpassed that of many adults. He had given me what I needed. I needed room for Roxanne to be *dying*.

Whatever we believe about the afterlife—or don't—we all need room to name it when someone is dying. We need room to be with people as they journey toward their death, surrounding those who are facing the end of their life or the death of loved ones with compassion and support. We need room to say, "She is dying," and to hear in response, "I'm here for you." We need room because our lives are full of dying and because dying takes room.

There is an official term for the grief I was feeling in this season. It's called *anticipatory grief*. This term was coined by grief researcher Erich Lindemann in 1944 and has become a part of our grief vernacular. Another author summarizes it this way: "Frequently . . . grief may have found its fullest expression before the death of this loved person. Its effects strike the bereaved-to-be at the moment the hopeless prognosis is pronounced, as he becomes aware of the truth of the situation. Therefore, the process of mourning begins long before the significant loss."

Roxanne had not yet died, but my grief had already started. When I went shopping with Roxanne, I was happy to be with her, but I was also grieving because our times shopping together were going to end. When I felt jealous about the time I couldn't spend with Roxanne, I was grieving all the time to come that I wouldn't be with my sister. When we went out for lunch, I remember it vividly because I was already mourning the end of lunches out together. Roxanne wasn't dead yet, but I already needed grieving room.

I am thankful for the moments the room was provided for me. Those moments looked like a lot of things. They looked like the congregants who donated air miles to cover the cost of one of my many flights home. They looked like friends who came over to pray one night—not for Roxanne but for *me*. They looked like the sweet prayer from my little boy. They looked like people saying, "How can we pray for you right now?" instead of instantly assuming we were still praying for a miracle.

And then one day, it looked like flowers.

On Easter 2013, Roxanne was dying. But I still had a resurrection sermon to preach because that's what pastors do on Easter Sunday. What could I possibly say? I talked about how when we bury someone, we lay flowers on a grave. I shared about different examples of death, and each time I did, I laid down another carnation, until two hundred carnations lay across the front of our church. I said these flowers reminded us of all the disappointments and deaths we face.

As I looked out at my congregation, I saw all kinds of deaths sitting in front of me. I saw the woman whose three-year-old grandson had died of cancer. I saw the woman who had given birth to a stillborn child. I saw the parent whose thirteen-year-old daughter had died twenty years before. I saw people who had lost parents, and siblings, and grandparents, and so many people they loved. I saw the empty spots where congregants I had cherished used to sit. And I saw people still healing from a painful divorce, and people who were sick with chronic illnesses every day, and people whose lives had veered off every course they had hoped to follow. I saw the heaviness of death everywhere—deaths I carried close in my heart and that I grieved with these people I loved.

Finally, I talked about how the hope of Easter was that death was not the end. I believed it—for them, at least. But I was struggling to find my own hope on that particular Sunday. The death of someone I loved was too close.

After the sermon, I asked the musicians to start playing some music, and as they did, I told people that today we were going to make a point. We were going to declare that death would not win. To do that, we were going to *pick the flowers back up.* We would remember that graves were not the end. None of the graves we had faced or would face were the end of the story. I would soon be laying my own flowers on my beloved sister's body, a reality that lingered in my heart with every word I spoke. The only thing I was trying to do in the moment was not think about it too much.

I told everyone that I wanted them to come to the front and pick up a flower, and then, after they left that day, I wanted them to give that flower to someone who needed hope. I pictured flowers being given out all over our city, reminders of hope to lots of people that needed it.

I should have been prepared for what would happen next. You have probably already figured it out. But I can honestly say that I didn't see the next thing coming.

As the music played and I stood at the front, watching people come and pick up their flowers, I suddenly noticed someone next to me. There stood a member of my congregation who had walked on the stage and was holding a carnation out to me. Stunned, I took it.

Then more people came. And more people came. People were giving their flowers to me. I soon found myself standing with an armful of flowers, each from someone who had picked me as the person with whom they wanted to share resurrection hope.

I wanted to push back on the flowers, say no thank you, tell them to give them to someone else. They were supposed to take them away—give them to someone who *really* needed them. But my church recognized something I sometimes had trouble articulating: I needed resurrection too. They were telling me, "We see you, and we know you need this."

In those few short minutes, they all gave me the room that I needed. Room for dying, and room for hope. Flower after flower.

4

ROOM IN THE VALLEY OF DEATH
FINDING SPACE FOR GOD IN THE DARKEST PLACES

I officiate a lot of funerals, and it's a very rare funeral where I am not asked to read Psalm 23. I know why people love to hear this reading in times of suffering and loss. The familiarity of this poem reminds us of the presence of God. In its most quoted version from the King James translation, it reads:

> The Lord is my shepherd; I shall not want.
> He maketh me to lie down in green pastures; he leadeth me
>   beside the still waters.
> He restoreth my soul; he leadeth me in the paths of
>   righteousness for his name's sake.
> Yea, though I walk through the valley of the shadow of death,
>   I will fear no evil; for thou art with me; thy rod and thy
>   staff, they comfort me.
> Thou preparest a table before me in the presence of mine
>   enemies; thou anointest my head with oil; my cup
>   runneth over.
> Surely goodness and mercy will follow me all the days of my
>   life, and I will dwell in the house of the Lord forever.

People of Christian faith, no faith, and any number of faith backgrounds take comfort from this passage. For years before Roxanne died, I had read and loved these words. But the truth of their promise did not truly become clear to me until I found myself in the valley of death's shadow with my own loved one.

Roxanne continued her steady decline when I returned to Ontario after my last visit. She had already decided that she wanted to spend her final days in a medical facility, which in St. John's meant the palliative care ward of a hospital. She wanted to have access to pain medication when she needed it, and she didn't want her family to have the memory of her dying at home. One night at the end of April, she decided the time had come. She declared to her husband, Mike, that she was ready to go. They made arrangements, gathered her things, and Roxanne left her home without hardly looking back.

She settled into the room that would be her final home, and we all had to join her in the valley of the shadow of death. This valley was a place I had visited often in my work as a pastor, but entering it with a sister was new to me.

When we walk in the valley of the shadow of death ourselves, we often notice things there we have never seen before, and I was discovering a lot of them for the first time.

In the valley, there is indecisiveness.

I simply could not decide what to do most days. Nothing ever seemed like the right thing. Everything seemed like the wrong thing.

It started with my obsession over when to return to Newfoundland. I did not want to miss being there when Roxanne died. At the same time, I had young children at home and a job, and I couldn't stay away for stretches that were too long. I didn't want to go to Newfoundland too soon and end up away from my kids for several weeks. I also didn't want to go back too late and miss the last days of Roxanne's life.

I thought about this nonstop. I would obsessively phone and text Mike, Mom, Jason, Darlene, and Deanne. "When should I come home?" I would ask over and over and over. "Whenever you think," they would answer. "I really want to be there when she dies," I would say. "Then you should come," they would answer. "But when is she going to die?" I would ask. "We can't answer that," they would remind me again. I wanted a timeline. I wanted a game plan. But with dying, there isn't one. The lack of control was infuriating.

"I can't leave too early," I would say to my husband. "Why not?" Dallas would ask. "Because I can't leave the kids too long." "They'll be fine," he would assure me. "I don't want to be a bad mom," I would explain. "Being with your dying sister doesn't make you a bad mom," he would remind me. It didn't feel that way.

"I can't take too much time off of work," I would say on other days. "The church must be getting frustrated with me." "No one feels that way," Dallas would assert. "I can't leave it all on your shoulders!" I would say to Dallas, again. "I'm fine," he would say, again.

"What do you want most right now?" Dallas would often ask me, trying to help me make the right choices for me. "I want to be a good sister," I would say, over and over and over. But then I would add, "And I want to be a good mom. And I want to be a good pastor. I don't know how to be all those things at the same time." "Nobody asked you to," Dallas would say.

Finally, I booked a flight home for May 2. Three days before I was set to leave, I paid a fee to change the flight to May 1. When I got to the airport, I paid another $150 to change my flight so that I landed at 9 pm instead of 2 am the next day. Nothing in particular had changed in Roxanne's health in that time, but somehow I couldn't shake the feeling I had to get it right. I was counting every hour, though counting down to what time, exactly, I couldn't say. I asked everyone what I should do, and no one could tell me. At the airport I even asked the airline attendant who was rearranging my flight if she thought I was doing the right thing.

When I landed that night and Roxanne's sister-in-law Diane met me at the airport, I asked her to take me straight to the hospital. She explained that Roxanne had been given a sedative at 8 pm and would be asleep until the next morning. Mike was heading home as we spoke. There was no point in going to visit.

I must have seemed a bit distraught because Diane put a hand on my shoulder and said, "Leanne, I know that you probably feel like you just want to see her. But right now, she is resting, and that is what she needs. Let me bring you to the house." I remember feeling grateful that someone was telling me what to do.

The reality was that there was no right thing to do, but that didn't stop the questions from coming. Was there some correct amount of time to be at the hospital? Was it okay to leave Roxanne for a few minutes? Was it all right to talk about normal things while she lay dying next to us? Even little things were hard. Should I take a walk, or should I not take a walk? Should we go out to eat or order in? Should I have fries or salad? Every question was difficult.

A lot of us have been there. How do we negotiate a world we have never seen before? The valley of the shadow of death is an indecisive, uncertain place. Psalm 23 suggests that, with the Lord as my shepherd, I would not want. But let me tell you, I *wanted*. I wanted clarity, and direction, and answers for all my questions. I didn't want the ambiguity that came in the valley.

I see now that this uncertainty is a feature of the valley of the shadow of death. When people are sitting with a dying loved one, I sometimes see them spiral over simple questions, like whether they want me to bring them a cup of coffee or whether I should visit in the morning or afternoon. "I just don't know what to do" is one of the most common things I hear.

This is such a normal part of death's valley. We *don't* know what to do. We don't know when we should visit, and we don't know when we should leave. We don't know whether it's okay to talk or if we should stay quiet. We don't know if we want soup or a sandwich. In the valley, we just *don't know*. And this makes sense. How can we be expected to negotiate the darkness of a valley like the valley of death? It's harrowing and confusing, and most of us have never been there before.

The valley is also a place of helplessness.

The day after my flight arrived, I walked into Roxanne's room bright and early. It was a glorious spring morning, and she was sitting up a little. She turned to me and said, "Hi, Sister. Nice top," and all of us in the room laughed, each of us a little stunned. There was the Roxanne we loved, still seeping through. I leaned in, hugged her, and then sat next to the bed as she drifted back to sleep.

What was I supposed to do next? Mike and Darlene opened crossword books, their go-to for passing the time in those days. Mom and Dad paced the room. After a few minutes, I took out a book to read. Sometimes Roxanne would wake for a moment. Her conversations were nonsensical. One day she looked at me intensely and said, "We have to remember the cornflakes for the hash brown casserole." Another day, we realized she was attempting to write on a chalkboard, teaching invisible students in the hospital room.

Sometimes she would want to eat a little and would manage a small slice of toast or some water to drink. We would all clamor to get it for her. Then we would sit and wait some more. If she needed to get to the bathroom, which was rare, Darlene or Mike would help her walk there and back, and she'd lie back in bed for another long stretch.

The doctors monitored her pain medication. We would watch as she dealt with her pain, trying to think of something to help her when she was obviously hurting. "Can you give her more?" we would ask. "She's at the highest dose now," they would remind us.

We were all helpless. We were powerless to make Roxanne feel better, unable to stop the semitruck of death barreling toward us. There weren't smoothies to buy anymore. There weren't last-ditch treatments to try. There weren't magic words to be said. There was no way to climb out of the valley.

One day Roxanne was feeling a little warm, and Darlene got a cold cloth from the bathroom and wiped her forehead. A few hours later, I was in the car with Mom and Dad on our way to get some food. My mom suddenly broke down. "I wanted to do the cloth!" she said. "I'm the *mother*! I should wipe her brow!"

I got it. We all shared that feeling of helplessness.

One of the hardest things to handle when someone we love is dying is accepting that we don't know what to do. Every day we want to *do* something. So we say, "Can I fluff your pillow? Can I wipe your brow? Can I find the right pain medication, figure out a good prescription, suggest the miracle cure you haven't tried?"

As we watch those we love journey with someone dying, we also try to find things to do. We offer to mow lawns, make meals, and babysit. We bring muffins, coffee, and gift cards. We say, "If there is anything I can do—*anything*—please do not hesitate to ask." And we mean it.

It is good to do things for those who are preparing for death. These things meant so much to us. But at some point, we realize that nothing we do will stop the inevitable. No meal to curb the loss. No gift card to end the suffering. No perfect words to say. Nothing. The valley is a helpless place.

The valley is crowded with a lot of things. There is desperation. There are voices still trying to convince us to "not give up," the people assuring us a miracle is still on the way, the eager insistence that the tide will turn, despite all the evidence pointing to the contrary.

One day my mom walked cheerfully into the family room at the hospital, declaring she had something to remind all of us. She had gotten a call the night before from someone eager to encourage her, a woman who had said, "I thought you were all Christians! I thought you should have faith! Why are you all giving up?"

"And she's right!" Mom said, adamant, defiant, back straight and chin up. "We can't give up! God can still *heal her!*"

We stared at her, dumbfounded. I resisted the strong urge to track down the person who had phoned and yell at them to stop giving my mom false hope. But I took a breath. We were all desperate, and it came out in different ways. Mom was desperate to pretend her daughter wasn't dying. Her friend was desperate to help her. "That was really nice of her to call you, Mom," I said, "But I don't think she realizes how sick Roxanne is."

"Well, I'm not giving up," she declared, rebuffed. Who was I to argue, when we all longed to be anywhere but the valley we were in? Who was I to say there couldn't be room for that desperation?

Who are any of us who want to find our own versions of hope wherever we can in the darkest moments of our lives?

In the valley, there is second-guessing. For us, there was "Maybe we should have tried one more trial," and "Maybe she should have stayed at home," and "Maybe she should have checked the spot on her head sooner eight years ago." For others, there is "Maybe we should try a different treatment," or "Maybe he needs a better doctor," or "Are we sure this is the right thing?"

In the valley, there is normal life. In our valley, we had takeout chicken for dinner (with mashed or baked potatoes?) and crossword puzzles ("Does anyone know a four-letter word for *awkward*?"). We had school runs to get the girls and drives to activities and hospital visits. We had homemade quilts on the hospital bed, long walks around the pond, and hockey playoffs on television. For you, there may be calls from work, chatty conversations, knitting, kids running around, jokes, arguments, and the weird sensation that life somehow keeps going while your world is imploding.

The valley is complicated. There is so much time and not enough. There is nothing to do but wanting to do something. There is sitting, pacing, fussing, fidgeting, speculating, crying, then waiting some more. All these things clamor for room, and all of them take their own space in their own way.

But of all the things that are hard in the valley, the thing that was worst for me was the suffering.

For Roxanne, the suffering looked like tumors. By the time she died, Roxanne had them everywhere. She had skin cancer, after all. That meant that besides the cancer ravaging her internal organs, it was growing all over her skin, tumors growing bigger and more dramatic every day. They were on her legs. On her arms. On her head, sticking out between the fluffs of gray hair that had started to grow back since the treatment had ended. On her beautiful face. They were red, they were raw, they were ugly. They were *everywhere.*

And they hurt. They were awful to look at, yes, but clearly they were much more awful to feel. Each time Roxanne moved, she'd wince, as one tumor or another sent pain searing through her body.

The wincing was what really got to me. My sister was on heavy painkillers, and they were doing their work, but when cancer is eating your body from the inside out and the outside in, there is a limit to what pain meds can do. A simple move in her bed or a turn of her head on her pillow would clearly send pain through Roxanne's body. We would see her reach up to touch her head, almost surprised, as the pain struck her again, see her flinch when even just a blanket touched the now enormous tumor on her leg. In the valley, it was that wincing that I hated most of all, the thing that made me want to run from the room and scream at God to make it stop.

For months, I couldn't picture those winces without crying. Couldn't talk about them. I would close my eyes at night and remember that look on her face as she suffered. To this day, the memory of those flinches is perhaps the worst memory of my life: the memory of the severe suffering my sister faced in the valley of death.

I didn't want to give the suffering any room at all. But it was unavoidable. The valley was full of it, and all we could do was sit as silent witnesses to its raging presence.

For many, suffering in the valley is what feels the darkest of all.

How little we know about the valley of the shadow of death until we sit in it, hour after hour, waiting as a loved one dies. How dark the shadow can feel. How much room the valley needs.

And how true, too, is this line from Psalm 23: "Even in the darkness of the valley of the shadow of death, *you are with me.*" I didn't know how much I would feel God near me in the valley, and I had no idea how sacred and holy the valley could be. This is often a great surprise.

God was in the lowland, too, along with all the awful things. I saw it every day in kind words and encouraging messages and people who brought us donuts or coffee or flowers. I saw it in the compassionate care of Roxanne's doctors and nurses and the way Mike cared for her so well. I saw it in the fact that, somehow, we woke up every day and walked back to that palliative care ward, put one foot in front of the other, sat by the shell of my broken sister's body, and kept breathing ourselves. It amazed me. How could this time have anything but pain? But it turns out there is room for more than heartache in the valley. There is also room for God.

I saw it most in the answer to the deepest longing of my heart: my prayer that I could bless my sister one more time. Moments alone with Roxanne were even more rare in the hospital than they had been at her house, and being by myself with Roxanne was still something I didn't feel like I could ask for from her family and friends. But I prayed for it every night as I lay in bed on the futon in Roxanne's basement. "One moment, God," I would ask. "One moment."

Then I got it. I hadn't planned it. Mike and Darlene had gone to get the children from school. Mom and Dad had headed home for the day. Miraculously, there were no other visitors. And there I was with my sister, in what turned out to be the last full day of her life, alone.

It didn't feel good. Alone with Roxanne, it was as if I could feel death creeping in to steal my sister from me. The valley was very deep. The shadow was all around me. There was so little left to do. But there was one thing I wanted. I wanted to sing a blessing over my sister.

We have a song we sing at our church as a blessing. I had originally come across the song on a lullaby CD someone had given to us for our children. The words are a Scripture verse set to a simple tune. As an infant, Lucy wouldn't go to sleep without the CD on repeat, and for years, every night before she went to bed, I would lay my hand over her face and sing this song as a final blessing before she slept. Now I laid a hand on Roxanne's sleeping arm, and I sang the words of blessing over her:

The Lord bless you and keep you
The Lord make his face shine upon you
And give you peace, and give you peace
And give you peace forever.

Roxanne slept through my singing. Her slow breathing never changed, and there was no glimmer of acknowledgment that she heard—no twinkle of an eye or squeeze of my hand. The trajectory of her death didn't turn. She was still dying, and it still hurt beyond any words. But I got to sing. And as impossible as it seemed, I felt God with me. God felt more real to me in that hospital room than in almost any other moment in my life. My world was coming undone with each of Roxanne's labored breaths—and there was God, in the shadow of the valley of death.

"Even as I walk through the valley of the shadow of death, you are with me. Your rod and your staff, they comfort me." A few years after Roxanne died, I did more research on the idea of the rod and the staff. Turns out shepherds in the ancient world, like the shepherds used in the image of this psalm, had two important tools. They had a big staff that looked like a giant hook or cane. We usually picture shepherds holding staffs. Kids in bathrobes are sure to have them in Christmas pageants. Shepherds used these staffs to pull sheep toward themselves in times of danger. The hook on the end could be used to pull in a wayward sheep or pick up a lamb that had fallen. The staff brought the sheep back to the shepherd. It kept them safe.

The rod was different. The rod was a short blunt instrument, like a small club. It was used to push the sheep in the ways they had to go. It might be used to push two sheep apart if they were fighting or to shove a sheep away from something that would harm them. It's unlikely the sheep would have liked the rod. It probably hurt, and it would have almost always felt unwanted.

And yet here the writer, thinking of God like a shepherd, says, "When I'm in death's valley, your *rod* and your staff comfort me." That intrigues me. To a sheep, the rod would never have felt comforting. The rod was painful. Yet the shepherd's love was there when the rod was at work just as much as when the shepherd used the staff. The rod hurt, but the shepherd wasn't any further away. The shepherd was still close.

Let me be clear about what I am not saying. I'm not saying that my sister's death was a kind act on God's part, that her suffering and dying were some version of the "rod" that God used to help my faith grow. This is a theological position I simply do not hold.

But I do see, as I look back on her dying, that in a time that was profoundly painful, God was, somehow, still there, pulling me close. God's comfort was present to me in the rod and the staff. I know many who have expressed the same reality, including those who would not call the hope they felt in life's darkest moments "God's presence." Some will talk of feeling "unexplained peace," or "a strange sense of comfort," or "a sense that something beyond us" was happening. Sometimes we don't have the language to quite describe the sense of something transcendent happening as death closes in, but we feel it. It can surprise, alarm, and comfort us to discover that a time shrouded by the ugliness of death can also somehow have great beauty. We don't talk about the beauty nearly enough.

Many spiritual writers have described certain places or times as "thin spaces." These are places or locations in which the space between earth and heaven seems more porous. Thin spaces are often described in the writings of Celtic Christianity in reference to creation. David Adam writes about the Celtic church: "They prayed that their eyes might be opened, that all their senses might be made alert to that which is invisible. They prayed that they might have the eagle's eye to see Him who comes at all times."

Although Adam is referring to the vigilance of Celtic Christians to discover God's presence in the beauty of nature, I believe we can also pray for open eyes in hospital rooms, palliative care wards, and cemeteries. Times of death and dying can be thin spaces, places where we can see the God who comes at all times. I felt that holy space in the days I waited for my sister to die, and I have felt it often since then.

A couple of years ago, I got a call from a member of my congregation whose wife had been in the hospital. She was nearly ninety, and her health had been steadily declining. It was not a surprise to hear that the doctors had said death was imminent. Her husband was calling to ask me to come and visit. Somehow I missed the call, however, and when I got the message, two hours had passed since he had phoned. I was angry with myself that I had missed the call and might be too late to pray with Anne before she died.

I rushed to the hospital and entered her room. Anne was surrounded by her husband, children, grandchildren, and great-grandchildren. I hugged them one by one, asked how everyone was doing. There were lots of tears for this much-loved woman. Anne would be missed deeply.

We gathered around her bed, and I read Psalm 23. As I said, "In the darkness of the shadow of death, you are with me," I knew it again to be true. I felt the comfort sweep the room. I shared a few words and prayed. And I asked if I could sing. Again, they nodded.

Standing there like I have done so many other times since Roxanne died, I laid my hand on Anne's forehead. This was another woman I loved. Anne had become a dear friend and mentor, and I had to fight to keep my voice even as I sang the song of blessing that is now part of my own last rites.

> *The Lord bless you and keep you,*
> *The Lord make his face shine upon you,*
> *And give you peace, and give you peace*
> *And give you peace forever.*

Once again, I felt myself standing in the thin space. Something sacred was all around us. The room was calm, and full of people, and full of love. Full of God.

As I was leaving the hospital, another member of our congregation was walking the hall, clearly upset. I asked what had brought her to the hospital that day. She explained she was visiting an old friend, a colleague, who was dying. "Maybe you know her," she said, telling me her name: Dawn Sherwood.

Although I didn't know her well, I did know Dawn. I knew that before my time, she had attended our church. Her daughter had attended on and off during my time at Mount Hamilton, and once in a while, her mom had come to church with her. I hadn't seen either of them in a long time. I had no idea Dawn was sick, far less that she was dying. Dawn's only son had died of cancer a few years before in his early twenties, and church had not come easily to Dawn after that.

I asked my congregant if she thought it would be okay if I visited Dawn. "Actually, she just mentioned she wanted a chaplain," she said, "And they haven't found one yet."

I found Dawn in her hospital room, alone, and hooked to machines. I leaned in close, reminded her who I was. She nodded, recognizing me. I asked if she wanted me to read something, if she wanted me to pray, and she offered a gentle nod.

For the second time that day, I read Psalm 23 over someone dying. For the second time, I prayed. And for the second time, I sang. By then, Dawn had drifted off to sleep. The room was dark, empty, and quiet. It was a very different scene than the one around Anne's crowded hospital bed. But I felt it again: God, there, in the valley of the shadow of death.

Later I messaged Dawn's daughter to let her know I had visited her mom. I found out that Dawn had died a few hours later. Turns out that I was the last person to pray with her.

Anne ended up living a few more days. So while I hadn't needed to worry about missing a last chance to be with Anne when I missed that phone call, it had made me just on time for Dawn.

Often in times leading up to death, we want to do all we can to avoid the valley. We are scared, we don't know what to do, and we don't know if we can cope. Sometimes that looks like refusing to visit someone who is dying because it is "too hard." Sometimes it looks like visiting a dying person and feeling like we still have to pray for them to get better. Sometimes it looks like forcing everyone around us to pretend that the dying person isn't really dying or that all of this isn't really so hard. I see it all the time. Because we do not see the sacred space that the space of dying can be, we avoid it in all the ways we can. We don't recognize the thin space before us. We don't make room for it.

Because of my job, I sometimes mention in passing to people that I am on my way to visit a dying person. "Oh, I am so sorry!" people say, or "How do you do that?" I never quite know how to tell them that, while I know it will be hard beyond words, I also know I am stepping into a hallowed place. I know that I will see God. I never know how to say that I almost look forward to those times—not because they will be easy but because God will be there.

When Roxanne was dying, a family friend who had grown up in Zimbabwe came to visit. Darlene described his moving visit to me one day when I was venting about how awkward it was when visitors only focused on Roxanne getting better. "His visit was nothing like that, Leanne. He walked in the room, and he got on his knees," Darlene told me. "And he didn't pray for Roxanne to be healed. He prayed for God to meet her at the gates. He prayed for her homecoming. Leanne," she said, "He prayed her into glory."

I knew this young man had seen more than his share of death in his life. He had not been shielded from the valley like most of us growing up in Canada had been. Because of that, he seemed to know that we did not need to fear the darkness but could seek God in it.

I often think of that man's prayer when I walk back into someone's dark valley of death with them. Sometimes when I walk into a room with someone dying, I remember those words: "Pray them into glory, Leanne," I think. Pray, and sing, and walk them into glory. The space is thin, and God is here.

You can also make this space in your dark valley. This doesn't mean that you dismiss how hard it is or pretend that what you're facing isn't the worst thing you can possibly imagine. It simply means knowing that there can be more than horror, and more than awful, and more than your very worst thing.

It means there can also be God, and peace, and something miraculous in the valley with you. And it's okay to give it room.

5

ROOM FOR IMPERFECT GOODBYES
LETTING GO OF MOVIE MOMENTS

I am not a fan of sentimental movies, so I was probably never going to like *The Christmas Shoes*. It is a full-length movie based on the song of the same name. In the song, a cynical man is looking for last-minute gifts on Christmas Eve when he notices a young boy looking at a pair of shoes. The boy explains that he wants to buy the shoes for his mom, who is going to meet Jesus that night. Turns out his mom has cancer, and he wants his mom to wear the shoes to heaven. The man buys the shoes for the boy, his heart is changed, there's Christmas joy, and blah, blah, blah.

Like I said, I was unlikely to ever like this movie, but I dislike it even more since my sister died. This is not because it involves a woman dying of cancer; it is because of the way the woman's death is presented. In the climax, the son runs home to his mom and gives her the shoes. She says a beautiful goodbye, and as the shoes are placed on her feet, she serenely slips away, a slight smile on her face. Now, I did tear up when I first saw that touching moment. But the image frustrates me because it epitomizes how deathbeds are often portrayed in movies or on television: Loved ones gather around a cognizant and coherent dying person. The dying person speaks meaningful words or gives special mementos just moments before they gently slip away.

Sometimes—*sometimes*—this happens. But "Christmas-shoe deaths," especially with people dying after a lengthy illness, are mostly unrealistic. And many people feel cheated when their last moments with their loved ones don't look like the scripted scenes they have come to expect.

That's why I believe we need room for the story of our loved one's last moments to not be ones of "closure" or poignancy. We need room for those endings to not to have a lot of apparent meaning, except to us. We need room for imperfect goodbyes.

Several years ago, I visited a congregant named Dan, who was in the last days of a horrible disease called Lewy body dementia. Dan had a huge family, and each time I visited, the room was full of different loving relatives—but always his wife, Joy, and often his son.

On the Saturday evening I visited, I found a few siblings and Joy sitting and chatting around Dan's bedside as usual. They told me the nurses suspected it would still be a couple of days before Dan died. But Joy took me aside and said, "I don't think it's going to be a couple of days. I think it's going to be sooner. I feel like I should call my son and tell him to come back tonight."

I didn't know why she thought that, but I sensed her anxiety that her son was not there. She could call him and say exactly what she told me, I suggested, and then her son could make a choice. If he felt like coming, he could. If not, that was his choice, too, and he could come back the next day, as planned. After all, the nurses had said it would be a few days. She smiled and agreed. That's what she would do. She left the room to call her son.

I sat down next to Dan, took his hand, and started chatting with a few of his sisters. We were making small talk when one of them asked, "Leanne, is he still breathing?" I paused and looked, and it became very obvious to me that he wasn't.

"Why don't you call the nurse?" I said, trying to project calm. The nurse rushed in and confirmed our suspicions. Just then Joy came back in the room after calling her son and quickly took in the scene. "Is he *gone*?" she cried. And he was. He had died in the very short window of time in which she had left the room, less than five minutes. I was the one person holding his hand, and I hadn't even noticed when he slipped quietly into the next life.

Later, Joy would muse that maybe Dan had waited for her to leave the room, saving her the pain of having her witness his death. This is, of course, possible. Still, it meant that Joy did not have a Christmas-shoes death story to tell. She had her own story, one she told over and over in the hours and days to come. How their pastor was the one holding his hand, how Dan would have liked that, how it was so peaceful when he died that no one had even noticed. How like Dan it was, to not make a scene.

It was very peaceful. But it was not the goodbye Joy wanted. She needed space for that imperfect death: the one where she wasn't even present when her husband died, the one she alone had known was closer than everyone else thought and so had called her son to suggest he join them.

Perhaps even more difficult for many is the reality of goodbyes for deaths that are completely unexpected. Saying goodbye to someone who is about to die after a sudden accident or heart attack, when there has been no time to prepare for death, is even more complicated. How could anyone ever be expected to say goodbye—with intention, or grace, or courage—to someone who had been living a normal life just a few hours before?

Then there are the goodbyes that simply don't happen at all: the death at the scene of the accident, the losses discovered via phone call or police visit. I can think of countless times that someone lost a person suddenly and later lamented to me, "I didn't get to say goodbye!" They would have given anything for even a moment at a deathbed instead of having a doctor or police officer tell them their loved one had died. They crave a Christmas-shoe moment.

The narrative of the "good goodbye" weighs heavily after these losses. But these types of "good goodbye" deaths are not as common as people assume. While some last goodbyes include family and friends gathered around a deathbed before their loved one contentedly closes their eyes and breathes a gentle last breath, I have never actually witnessed this. Most often that final deathbed scene is one simply of waiting, of watching a person who has been sick slip away or sometimes wrestle to the very end.

Although idyllic goodbyes are rare, we can feel deprived or even guilty when we don't have them. I have talked to so many people who wondered if they did something wrong because they didn't have that last "special' conversation with their loved one just before they died. They feel robbed of what they thought deathbed moments should look like.

But we need to make room for goodbyes to look like a lot of things. Our person's death may look nothing like a poignant movie scene, and we still need room for it. We need room for goodbyes to happen in many different ways. Sometimes in a gentle moment of blessing. Sometimes at funeral homes. Sometimes months later, at a graveside. Sometimes in a moment that is just for the person grieving, when they find their own way to let go. We need room for all these endings.

I had just crawled into bed in Roxanne's basement. We had been at the hospital all day, and we had been told that Roxanne would probably die within the next twenty-four to forty-eight hours. The nurse had pointed out the "mottling" on her legs. Those white and red discolored circles meant her body was shutting down, a shutdown that was going to keep moving toward her organs until her body was all done. Her hands were already getting colder as we held them.

I was so tired. I had done nothing but sit at a hospital all day, but I was exhausted. Mike and Darlene had planned to stay for the night shift. Jason, his wife, Lana, and I went home. "Call us if anything changes," we told them. The girls were at a youth retreat, as we tried to continue to keep life as normal as we could for them in the midst of the chaos.

I was drifting off to sleep when the phone rang, and without even waiting for Lana to come and get me, I got up and started to put on my clothes. I knew the final shadow was imminent.

One of the greatest longings of my heart had been to be there when my sister died. I knew it wasn't mine to expect or ask or control.

People die on their own schedule. People die in rooms that are empty despite everyone's efforts to be there. People who want to be present don't arrive in time. Sometimes people step out for five minutes and miss the moment of death after months of never leaving someone's side. I was worried that would happen to me, but in the end, I received my desire at 11:55 on a Saturday night.

We held her hands, like people do. The whole ward was quiet, the room quieter still. Jason turned on the hockey game, and I took out my book. We all settled in, expecting it to still be hours before Roxanne actually died. She had eaten toast that morning. She had actually gotten out of bed. The doctor said he had not seen anything quite like it for someone at her phase of her illness. We laughed at that. That was Roxanne, ever the overachiever.

Now we sat, and we held her hands, and we listened to her breathing. As the time between breaths lengthened, we turned the game off, and I put down my book.

Her breath was labored, shallow, barely there. She was asleep and comfortable. It was gentle, and beautiful, and devastating. There was raspy breath after raspy breath, until there simply wasn't any more.

"Is that it?" Jason asked.

"I don't know," I said.

He leaned in close, trying to hear if her breathing had stopped. We still weren't quite sure. "Do we need a mirror?" I asked.

I was serious, but when Jason looked at me with his eyebrows raised, I realized how crazy it sounded. Yes, I had just suggested finding a mirror to hold up to my sister's nose to assess if she was breathing. We decided that instead of a mirror we could just get the nurse.

The nurse came in and gently took Roxanne's hand. She looked at us, and, without saying a word, she nodded. That was when the sobs started, hard. That was when we wailed, hugging her body as tightly as we had longed to do for weeks, when it had been too physically painful for Roxanne for us to do so. The nod told us her body was done and we could let all the feelings fly at last. But even as I saw it, my mind flashed back to a nod I had seen just a few weeks before, from a man who kept nodding his head as I sang at the Good Friday service:

In life, in death, Oh Lord, abide with me.

There were no Christmas shoes. It was imperfect and right.

After Roxanne died, we each took a few minutes alone with her. When I was with her, I took her hand and cried over her body, snuggling in as close as I could from the side of her bed. I told her I loved her. I told her she was the best sister I could ever ask for. I put my head on her heart, and I wept until my brother came in and laid a hand on my shoulder, and we cried together.

Those of us who were there gathered to cradle her body one more time, gave final kisses, touched her face. Eventually, we were ready to leave. It turned out that we did know when it was time to walk away. We knew when it was time to leave behind Roxanne's body, along with all the ideas we had of what might happen when she died.

Many months later, I had another goodbye moment. I was sitting on a beach in the Bahamas, on a last-minute getaway Dallas's parents had suggested we take to honor our tenth anniversary. Overall it was a good trip, a time to rest, and connect, and enjoy good food and long naps after a really hard year. But Roxanne's death was still all around me. I was still in the throes of grief.

It was nearing the end of a windy day, and white-capped waves were crashing along the pristine sand. We had gone parasailing that day, and to my surprise, I had felt happy. While Dallas went back to our room to clean up for dinner, I lingered on the beach. I sat near the water's edge and let the waves wash over me, relishing the rush of the water each time it covered my legs and then washed away again.

And then suddenly I was crying. My grief was there, crashing into me like the warm Bahamian water.

I began making patterns in the sand and watching the waves wash them away, one design after another, when I found the patterns turning to words. I wrote *cancer*. And then the waves came and washed the word away. I wrote *melanoma*, and the waves came again, making that ugly word also disappear. I wrote word after word, my index finger getting caked in mud as I wrote *broken, anger, death*. I remember the tears coming hard when I wrote the word *tumors*, those vestiges of horror I had so longed to take from Roxanne and never could.

The waves flowed and flowed, and the words came and came, and my tears fell and fell until finally I wrote *Roxanne*. I sobbed, and the waves swept her name away.

Those were my goodbyes. Imperfect ones. And they were good. They were meaningful. They were *mine*. These are the goodbyes for which I needed room.

There is room for your goodbye. There is room for screaming goodbyes over a casket, raging goodbyes over a body not found, goodbyes said to someone who can no longer hear them. Goodbyes without the "I love you" you had always hoped to hear or say. With or without Christmas shoes, you can find room for your perfectly imperfect goodbyes.

6

ROOM FOR THE RITUALS
WHY WE ALL NEED A GOOD FUNERAL SUIT

Shortly after I started working at my church, I was shopping with a friend and trying on a new suit. It was not the type of suit most women my age would choose. But I was a couple of years into my role as a pastor, and, as one well-meaning congregant had once pointed out to me, I needed to "build my professional wardrobe."

The modest, gray skirt and blazer were perfect for my role. "This is such a great suit for funerals!" I said to my friend as I came out of the changing room. Next to me, a woman made a startled sound, and I turned to see a stranger looking at me in disbelief. I realized that perhaps she thought I had recently had a loved one die. "Oh, it's okay, I'm a minister," I clarified.

This did not help things.

She shook her head, rolled her eyes, and turned away in obvious disgust. Then it came to me: the issue was not her concern that I was grieving. It was that I had said the word *funeral*—this word that clearly did not belong in the store where she was trying to shop.

In the years since that incident, I have become more aware of this annoyance at the mention of death or things surrounding it, this sense that grief is not an appropriate topic. Our culture has become increasingly death-avoidant. Bad-feeling-avoidant. Grief-avoidant. People say things like:

> "We aren't going to have a funeral; it would be too sad."
> "We won't bother with visitation. It will be too hard on everyone."
> "We aren't going to have tears. We are going to celebrate their *life!*"

I get it. It's reasonable to want to sidestep hurting. It makes sense to think that if we skip the things that our culture does to mark a death, it would help us somehow skip some of our grief. So sometimes we don't have funerals. We encourage people not to cry because "they wouldn't want you to be sad." We use euphemisms like "passed away" or encourage younger people to stay away from the funeral as it will be "too much for them." We try to avoid the pain of grief by avoiding things that seem painful. Who can blame us?

But I want to say this clearly: if you are a grieving person, you need to make room for the rituals of death. Amanda Held Opelt speaks to this reality well in her book *A Hole in the World: Finding Hope in Rituals of Grief and Healing.* Written after a series of difficult losses in her life, including the sudden tragic death of her well-known sister, Rachel Held Evans, Opelt explores and esteems the values of grieving practices from a range of traditions and cultures. I join in her lament that we have lost many of our collective grieving rituals; we are the lesser for it. She invites people to make room for rituals that include wearing black, tolling bells, and delivering casseroles as ways to help process grief. "Let's not move too quickly along as we do with so many of our hurts and discomforts these days," Opelt writes. "Could we creatively engage and discern together new ways to move our bodies into motions of grief?" Like her, I am eager to help people receive the gifts that rituals can offer us, making space for the many ways that this can look.

Avoiding rituals will not help make grieving easier. It can even make it more difficult. In our attempts to rush through grieving, we actually end up doing ourselves and others a dis-service. Not only do we miss a chance to honor the person who died, we also neglect an important opportunity to process our own emotions about their death. We need rituals to help us cope, celebrate, and grieve.

"Blessed are those who mourn, for they shall be comforted," Jesus said. He spoke this line as part of a collection of teachings when he describes being blessed in a lot of ways that are surprising. He says the poor are blessed, and the persecuted too. And he says those who are grieving are blessed. Nothing feels blessed about grief. Mourning does not feel like a blessing. Yet somehow it is true that we can be blessed as we mourn. This does not mean that mourning in and of itself is good. Instead, I believe this line speaks to a great truth: that in something that we assume will only be painful, we can still find peace. It is in making space for grief—not in avoiding it—that we find the comfort we so desperately want.

I found great solace in the rituals we did for Roxanne, as hard as most of them were to face. I dreaded every one of them and almost always wanted to skip them. Yet once I experienced them, I always found consolation because grace shows up when we make room for the rituals.

I was comforted by the times of visitations in the funeral home. I met parents of Roxanne's students, who wept and said no one had loved their child like Roxanne did. I met friends from years before and coworkers who were heartbroken, which made me feel less alone. Others were devastated too. Others knew that it didn't make sense for the world to keep spinning when Roxanne was dead.

People also made me laugh. When I met one of Roxanne's col-leagues, she gasped, commenting, as many people do, on how much I look like my sister. Slowly she reached her hand to my face and began pushing my cheek in with her finger. It suddenly dawned on me that she was trying to recreate Roxanne's dimple! She didn't even realize she was doing it. "You look *so* much like her," she said, pushing on my cheek, trying to conjure up one more image of her lost friend. I could almost feel Roxanne laughing next to me.

Moments like these would make us laugh so hard as we gathered each night to debrief the day. They were a grace, a gift, the room we needed to remember her. They were part of the blessing of mourning.

I felt loved through the funeral. My children at the time were just two and five years old. In Newfoundland, we didn't have access to babysitters we knew who wouldn't also need to attend the service. I had wondered what we would do. A few days before, I got a call from my friends, Jan and Jill, twins I had known since I was born. They explained to me that they had each taken the day off work so they could babysit my children during the funeral. I will never, ever forget this kindness. They were making room for our rituals, and in so doing, they made room for my grief. I felt swallowed up in compassion. I felt it again: the blessing as we mourned.

As the day of the funeral approached, I was almost sick with anxiety, so much so that the night before, my family insisted I take one of Roxanne's remaining sleeping pills to get me through the night. The next day, I still didn't know if I could face the service. When the time came, we gathered in the foyer of the church, ready to follow the casket into the sanctuary. When the doors opened, I gasped. There was a sea of people. I walked down the aisle and was surrounded by faces I knew and didn't know, tears streaming down all our cheeks. It was like an honor guard had formed as my sister was wheeled into her church one last time. There was blessing all around me.

At the graveside, I made one request. It is common in many Christian traditions to scatter sand on a casket as the officiant says the words, "This is ashes to ashes, dust to dust." I asked if I could scatter the sand on Roxanne's casket before it was lowered into the ground. As the pastor read the words of committal, I took the sand and poured the grains in the shape of a cross over the body of my cherished sister, declaring that, even in her death, she still belonged to God. That her body would be buried, but that she would rise to new life. It was painful. It was devastating. It was sacred.

But the greatest gift was when I got to share the eulogy, the one I had promised I would share and, as I had jokingly told her, "show right off." Really, I just wanted to make her proud. I wanted to remind everyone of this most incredible woman and what we would always remember about her. I shared about the sister I had adored as a little girl, the cool sister who traveled the world and was always off on adventures. I talked about how I could never wait for Roxanne to come home. I shared about the person who bossed us all around but whose lead we loved to follow. I described the parties she threw, and the gifts she gave, and the children's Christmas pageant she led every year at her church. I shared about how she was an amazing teacher, and a devoted mother, and a wonderful friend. I talked about how she inspired us. I ended with these words:

> When my daughter was born, I named her Lucy Roxanne, as a celebration of the bravery and strength Roxanne had shown. I think of what I will tell Lucy about what it means to be named Roxanne. I will say this: Lucy, I hope that like your Aunt Roxanne, you will be generous with your time and your resources and your love. I hope you will live with open hands and find joy in giving because you know life is better shared. I hope you will love people and see what's beautiful about everyone. I hope you will look out for people others overlook. I hope you will know how to have fun, how to live life to the fullest and to see joy all around you.
>
> I hope all these things for Roxanne's namesake, but if I had to say just one thing to her, it would be this: I hope you will be a good sister—because the one after whom you are named, Roxanne, was the best one anyone could ask for, which was why as a young child I could never wait for her to come home.
>
> And now, Roxanne, you are the one waiting at home, off on another adventure before I am. You will wait for us, and I know you are getting the party ready. I'll see you when I get there.

There was silence when I was finished, broken only by the sound of one strangled cry from somewhere in the crowd. I moved back to my seat, passing Roxanne's casket, and I could almost hear her whisper, "Well, you sure showed right off with that one."

And I knew it to be true again: *Blessed are those who mourn, for they shall be comforted.*

We need room for the rituals. In the rituals, we will find healing, even as they are hard beyond imagining. They carry us in the early days, and they often help us process as the days go on. I know that my experience of Roxanne's funeral was unique to our situation. But whatever your personal situation is, don't be afraid to make room for the rituals, whatever that looks like for you. Maybe it is a traditional funeral. Maybe you will find new ways to do things that work for your circumstance. But as challenging as it is to face the rituals of grief, I believe it is almost always harder not to.

There are good reasons people feel hesitant about some of these rites of passage. Some people fear a funeral because the attendance will be low. Some fear it because they do not want to face family drama and conflict that they are sure will come with it. Some simply do not want to deal with all the sadness. I know that I was fortunate to mourn for someone who had a full funeral and who had many who wanted to join in grieving for her. This is not true for everyone, and most people's funerals will look nothing like Roxanne's did. The combination of her personality, her early death, our huge family, and Newfoundland culture meant that her funeral and visitations were very large. But the size of the ritual does not change its importance.

I once officiated a funeral for a man who died with few people in his life. There were no children or grandchildren, and most of his friends had already died. He told his wife not to bother with a funeral because there wouldn't be anyone there. But a few weeks after his death, his widow felt she needed a way to say goodbye in an intentional way. Together, we planned a service that was simple and true to the things that her husband believed. She invited a few of her friends to join us. There were less than a dozen people there, including me and the pianist.

This funeral was no less important than Roxanne's. His wife told me afterward that it was a turning point in her healing. She felt the care of the few friends who had attended. I am convinced that even if it had just been her sitting in an empty church with me leading a service, she would have felt the ritual was healing for her. Rituals are *that* important.

When I went to camp as a kid, we used to do a chant called "Going on a Bear Hunt." The refrain of the chant, said as we smacked our legs in rhythm, went, "Going on a bear hunt. Gonna catch a big one. We're not scared!" After each refrain, a leader would then shout out an obstacle: "Oh no! Mud!" or "Oh no! A river!" Then the chant would continue: "We can't go over it. We can't go under it. We can't go around it. We've got to go *through* it." This would be followed by excited actions of trudging through mud or swimming through the lake.

I frequently bring up this chant, which has been turned into a popular children's book, when I am talking to grieving people who say things like, "I think we should forego a service" or "We just don't want people to be sad." I see what people are doing: they want to go around grief. I hear the pain, and I would love to take it from them. I would love it if something as simple as skipping a ritual would make grief go away or keep the sadness at bay. But as I hear the longing in those words of avoidance, I gently ask if they know the old camp song "Going on a Bear Hunt."

If they know the story, they get it right away. If they don't, I summarize it briefly. "You can't skip your grief," I tell them. "I know you want to. But you can't go over it. You can't go under it. You've got to go *through* it. That is the only way to the other side."

You won't avoid grief by avoiding the rituals. You won't escape pain by skipping the ceremonies. As hard and unmanageable as they may be, the rituals make space for your mourning. That's why they need room.

Perhaps as you read this you are thinking of rituals you missed that you now see you needed: the funeral you didn't have, the burial you left to others, the stories you remembered but didn't say out loud. It is never too late. There is still sand on seashores, still words that can be written, still honor that can be given. There is still room for your rituals.

Or perhaps you recognize your own attempts to help your loved ones skip their grief when you die someday. Perhaps you have told them not to have a funeral or not to be sad when you die. Your intentions are good, but people won't heal from their grief by evading it. They heal by living it. One gift you can give to your loved ones is helping them make room for rituals that will help them move forward.

When Jesus taught about the beatitudes, he turned the idea of blessing upside down. He was painting a picture of a blessed life that could be available to the most unlikely people. Blessing, he was saying, wasn't just for those who were rich. It wasn't just for those without problems. It could be found in poverty, in peacemaking, in suffering. And it can be found in mourning—if we make room.

So make room for some rituals, in whatever ways make sense for you. Remember that they don't have to look only one way. When people meet me to plan funeral services, I often tell them simply, "There aren't rules here." Yes, I can give advice on what usually happens and offer some insight into how certain things might work best, but I also remind them that variations are fine. Your family hates singing? Fine. No singing. You want to include a slideshow, a favorite poem, a room full of pictures? Of course you can. Ten different people want to speak? Why not?

I know a family that was hesitant to share their memorial request with their very traditional minister. Their father loved fireworks, and his one desire was that his family set off fireworks after his funeral. To their surprise, the minister thought it was a great idea. He arranged for everyone to gather in a small field near the church after the service, where we all watched a lanky teenager set a single firecracker off in the air as a tribute to his granddad. We loved it. I once worked with a family that wanted to give out their mom's favorite treat, saltwater taffy, for people to enjoy as her son sang "The Sound of Music," another favorite of his mom's. People were delighted. Of course, many religious traditions have set services for a funeral or memorial. In this case, you can include elements that are special to you at a reception, or at your home, or at a gathering at another time.

The rituals can look like something no one has seen before, or they can look like how rituals in your culture or tradition have looked for hundreds of years. However they manifest for you, what matters in the ritual is the space it makes for your loved one to be remembered, for you to process your loss, and for the world to bear witness to your grief. Formal funeral mass at a church, relaxed memorial at a funeral home, or scattering of ashes in the sea—the rituals all have one thing in common. They are part of giving you, and others, grieving room.

7

ROOM FOR THE GRIEF BUBBLE
ADJUSTING TO A LIFE MARKED BY LOSS

A few years ago, when our family visited the United Kingdom, we explored several medieval castles. One of our favorites had a room set apart where you could try on armor like knights would have worn centuries before, including their helmets. As I placed a helmet over my face, the sound in the room faded slightly, and the light grew a bit dimmer. Suddenly shielded from the rest of the room, I felt the sensation of being barricaded from the world. Separate.

And I realized that I recognized it. It was something that I often felt in the early days of my grief—an emotional barrier between myself and people around me that left me feeling separate and apart. It is something that many of us experience when we are grieving, when we live in what I now call the "grief bubble."

After someone we love dies, the world changes for us, and our place in it shifts. We become disoriented in familiar territory, foreigners to the life we had once known. We live in a bubble, a space where our loss is all we think about. It surrounds everything we do. We see, hear, and process everything with a slight distance between ourselves and others, floating in a bubble where our grief takes up all the air. We feel removed from anything but our grief.

People give it different names. I've heard people call it the "grief cloud" or the "grief fog." "There is a sort of invisible blanket between the world and me," Christian author C. S. Lewis says in his classic book *A Grief Observed*, written after the loss of his wife to cancer. "I find it hard to take in what anyone says. Or perhaps, hard to want to take it in." Blanket or bubble, it describes the same thing.

I was surprised by the bubble because I thought I was ready to grieve. When a loved one dies slowly, of cancer or another terminal illness, we might convince ourselves that we are prepared for grief. After all, we knew it was coming. We had time to prepare. I had already been grieving in so many ways leading up to Roxanne's death that I figured I had a head start on grieving. Maybe it would not be quite as hard for me as I knew it could be for others.

I could not have been more wrong. I quickly discovered that nothing had prepared me for the heaviness of deep grief. The bubble took me totally off guard. How did grief own every moment of every day? How was it *everywhere*? Why hadn't anyone warned me? Why hadn't I listened?

At first, there was just so much to do. No one really tells you how much *work* there is after someone dies. For the first few days, there is the funeral to arrange, the picture boards to make, the messages to send, the vendors to pay. There's "Did anyone call Uncle Frank?" and "Who is going to drive in the lead car?" and "I need to get my suit dry-cleaned for the funeral." It's a lot.

Then in the days after the funeral, there are casserole dishes to return, thank-you notes to write, paperwork to do. There are so many affairs to settle: insurance forms, and death certificates, and cleaning out the hospital supplies from your house. In our case, most of this work fell on Mike, of course. The hardest task on my plate was helping go through Roxanne's clothes. A few days after the funeral, we planned to gather again at Mike and Roxanne's house for a meal, after having spent a few days at my parents'. Even the idea of returning to her house was overwhelming. I dreaded walking back in the doors.

I wondered if it was still okay to call it "Mike and Roxanne's" when one of those people wasn't alive anymore. I was nervous about even going to St. John's, the city where Roxanne no longer lived.

I vividly remember the moment I walked into that much-beloved house, a second home to me, and opened the hall closet. I cried out and buckled over. The closet was practically empty! Where were all of Roxanne's coats? Where were all her shoes, her scarves, her hats? A closet that was usually jammed full of clothes was suddenly strikingly bare, with a few stray jackets hanging among a slew of empty hangers.

Mike heard my startled noise and met me in the hall. "I thought you could all go through Roxanne's clothes today," he explained. He had taken all her clothes and laid them on his bed for me and Deanne to sort through before we left. He didn't want us to miss the chance to take things that might mean something to us when we each returned to our homes.

It was a thoughtful thing to do—the right thing to do, really—but I wasn't ready. Couldn't Roxanne's house look just as it always had for a little longer yet? How could we get rid of her so quickly? But this was the task before us, a task that many other grieving people had completed before me and had dreaded as much as I did.

For three hours, we went through every item of her wardrobe, seeing what fit, deciding what we wanted to keep. Roxanne was smaller than me and Deanne, so many things had to be passed on. Mike began putting unwanted things in bags to take to the thrift store. I wanted to save everything. Roxanne had kept things for so long. She held onto things in case they came back in style or she needed them for a costume. She had original Doc Martens she had bought in the 1990s. She had clothes from the '80s that would have made any hipster swoon. How could we give these things away?

I felt myself start to panic, looking at the bags of clothes piling up. "We can't just get *rid* of it all," I cried, my breath heightened, tears starting to fall. Mike gently put his hand on my shoulder. "Leanne," he said. "You know how much your sister loved thrift stores and finding a great deal. Imagine someone going to a thrift store and how happy they will be to find some of these things. Just like Roxanne would have been."

He was right, and that thought gave me peace. Sometimes I still smile at the thought of whoever found those Doc Martens at the Salvation Army. Still, I scavenged all I could, justifying that things too tight and too short fit *well enough*. There was the top we bought together on one of her visits. There was the dress we bought at an outlet. We discovered that she had a whole bunch of shoes that were sizes too big with tissues stuffed in the toes to make them fit. We assumed she had found them on sale and couldn't pass them up. We laughed so hard at that. And then I cried because I couldn't tease her about the tissues in her shoes. Because I couldn't laugh with her about how she couldn't pass up a good deal.

And there were things I couldn't take, could barely look at. Like the suede blazer we had bought on our last shopping trip together. Like the things we discussed her wearing in her casket. These were too painful. These would have to stay in the closet for someone else whether they fit me or not.

Every five minutes or so, I would find my emotions welling over. "I can't do this," I would say out loud, for the tenth or fiftieth or hundredth time, sitting back on the bed again. Roxanne and I had spent so much time shopping together. Every item was full of a memory. Darlene and Deanne would encourage me to keep going, and slowly the pile on the bed got smaller and smaller.

I went home with two extra suitcases filled with T-shirts, and sweaters, and shoes, and purses I would barely use, lugging the lingering pieces of Roxanne across a country. For weeks, I would try something on, only to realize that it truly did not fit. And for months, I would fold them up again, put them back in my drawer, unable to throw out any more pieces of Roxanne. I didn't care about the person finding a deal at the thrift store. I cared about *me*.

The other tasks added to the work of grief. I had to write thank-you notes. This meant I had to go to a store to buy the cards. What ones should I buy? What are appropriate "my sister is dead, and you were really helpful" thank-you notes? I wanted to photocopy the bulletin from her funeral to include. That was a thing people did, right? What photocopier could I use? I had to find words to express my thanks, knowing that I never could. Over and over I simply wrote, "I don't have words to say how much what you did meant to me."

And I had to arrange my flight home. I had to let the church know my plan for return to work. I had to catch up on weeks' worth of emails. I had to update people about what happened. I had to reply to the well wishes.

And I still had to read bedtime stories, and make breakfast each morning for my children, and get out of bed each day—all of which felt like a lot. Grief is a lot of work, all around, all the time; a bubble of exhaustion.

Figuring out how to tell people what happened to you is complicated too. How do you announce that your father, or best friend, or child just died? When I got back to Hamilton, I couldn't figure out how to tell people what had happened. How would I announce that I was grieving?

I went to a parent council meeting for my son's school three weeks after Roxanne died. I remember considering that perhaps I shouldn't go but then thinking, "Why *wouldn't* I go?" I had no concept for how to manage my new life as a grieving person, so I mostly just went through the motions.

The meeting was awkward. My son was new to the school, and we didn't yet know anyone well, so no one there was aware of what I was going through. The whole time I kept thinking, "Do I tell them? Do I say, 'My sister died three weeks ago'?" I went around and around the question in my bubble of indecisiveness. I didn't know how to say it. I didn't want to bring everyone down, so I ended up saying nothing.

When the meeting was done, however, I felt like a fraud. I beat myself up for days afterward. How could I have been so disingenuous? How could I not mention that my sister died? How could I live like things were normal, even for an hour? And also, how could these women not notice that I was not, well, quite right? Did I seem okay? How could that be possible? Was the bubble so invisible?

When I did work up the nerve to tell people, I discovered that people did not know how to react to hearing a thirty-five-year-old woman say her sister had died. I began to brace myself for the stunned reactions I would receive to the news. The response was consistent. "Your *sister* died?" people would ask, aghast. "Your *sister?*"

"Yes, my sister."

Then would come the next question: "How old was she?" I saw what was happening. I watched people trying to process that something so significant could happen to someone *our* age. Then, when I would tell them that Roxanne was forty-eight, thirteen years older than I was, a ripple of relief would often spread over their faces.

"Oh, forty-eight," they would say, feeling a little better; she was not *quite* as young as they might have thought.

I hated that voice of relief. "Is it better for you now?" I so often wanted to respond. "Does this make it less difficult for you to process, now that you know she wasn't quite as young as you thought?" Her age certainly didn't make my grief easier. My big sister was dead. What difference did it make how old she was?

Sometimes people would follow up with another line I grew to dislike: "I can't imagine." "I can't imagine losing my sister," I heard over and over. "I can't *imagine* going through that," they would say. Again, I learned to bite my tongue. I learned not to say, "Lucky you. It's nice that you don't have to imagine. How lovely that you get to live in a world where the idea of your sister dying takes imagination." Sometimes I wished people would try to imagine. I wished they would try harder to think of what I was going through instead of saying that they couldn't. I wished that I didn't feel jealous of people who "couldn't even imagine" what I was trying to live through, how different it made me from them.

I hated having to face my grief afresh every time somebody else processed it for the first time. I loathed being a sad story. I detested being a person going through this big thing. I resented being someone grieving. Most of all, I hated that grief was everywhere, that my grief hung around me like a cloud I couldn't escape.

When we are grieving, it feels like we are floating in grief, swimming in grief, being consumed alive by our grief. It is all pervasive. The grief bubble is a hard home.

Nights were the hardest. One day my husband commented that he worried about leaving me home alone at night (which he often had to do as he picked up the slack on all the church meetings I was missing). He didn't want to leave me because he knew that a night home alone with my thoughts meant that I would turn to the worst of my grief. He knew he would come home to a partner in pieces. I didn't know what to tell him. I hated nights alone too.

Mornings were hardest. I suddenly found I was waking up earlier than I ever had to a quiet house. I watched so many sunrises, wishing that my heart would rise with the sun, only to find that it never did.

Days were the hardest. I could not believe how sad I was all the time. I couldn't believe I was expected to live with such heavy sorrow while a normal life continued. I desperately wanted the world to give me a grief hiatus. Couldn't everything just *stop* for a few weeks so I could do nothing but stay in bed and cry? I felt guilty for being a terrible mother. I felt like an awful pastor. I couldn't manage anything. I needed to sleep a lot. I was hundreds of miles away from Roxanne's home, and yet she was everywhere. There was the book she gave my kids, sitting on a shelf. There was the song from the funeral, being sung at church. There was the friend raising money for a cancer fundraiser, the disease that still consumed my life.

It felt like no one understood how hard it was. One friend told me that another friend commented that I seemed "distracted." It was accurate. After all, I lived in a bubble now. This meant that I was constantly distracted by grief, unable to engage in conversation, always a little distant from everyone.

I grew convinced that the pain would never get any better, ever. One night I sent a message to a friend whose sister had died a few years earlier, asking simply, "Does this ever get any better?"

"Better?" she responded. "I don't think it ever gets better. But right now, your grief feels like a wave. Each time it comes, it feels like it will drown you. But you will learn to ride the waves. The waves will keep coming, but when they do, you will ride them."

I wondered if I could ever learn to do that. I had been hoping she would simply answer with "Yes, it will get better," and I felt let down. Why did it have to be so complicated? I just wanted to know when I could step out of the bubble and back into the rest of the world again.

I arranged to order a ring. I had received some financial gifts to honor Roxanne, and I decided that I would use them to get something that would help me remember her all the time. I picked out a beautiful ring and asked the clerk to have the stone in it changed from sapphire to aquamarine, Roxanne's birthstone. The jeweler pushed back—the sapphire, he insisted, was perfect in the ring. It would look much better than an aquamarine stone. Finally I had to explain that I was buying a memorial ring for someone who had died. It was awkward. There was the pity face again, the questions: "Who was it? How old?"

"My sister."

(Gasp.)

"Forty-eight."

(Relief, again.)

Couldn't it ever *stop?*

I looked forward to getting the ring, convinced that it would bring some comfort and make Roxanne feel close to me again. When the day arrived, I put it on my finger and waited. Nothing. I felt frustrated. I had the ring, and I didn't feel any better. Roxanne still felt far away, even as her death was somehow everywhere. What could I possibly do for this to end?

I was less patient with everyone. I could not muster up the strength to care about people's problems. "Do people not realize that my *sister* has *died*?" I often thought. I didn't care about my friends' lives. I didn't care about suffering in the world. I only cared about my grief. I poured my heart out in my journal, day after day: "You know what the sucky part of grief is?" I wrote. "That all versions of the story still end with Roxanne being dead."

People felt farther away. I felt distant from the world, as distant as if I was wearing a heavy helmet over my head, one that divided me from those around me. It was like I was in my own universe, with just me and my grief.

Room for the grief bubble can be some of the hardest space to give someone else who is grieving because grieving people can seem hopelessly selfish. It can be hard to be the friend of a grieving person because you can feel like you have lost someone as well. And you have, in a way; you have lost your friend, for now, to grief.

A woman, now in her fifties, once told me that when her sister died at age eleven, she also "lost Mom for a year." Her mother was in the grief bubble, and no one could get in. A couple of years after losing Roxanne, my best friend told me that she felt like I was gone for a year too. I was with her, yes, but I was also in my bubble.

You may be in a grief bubble right now. Maybe you feel like you have been there for a while. You are still seeing your loved one around every corner, feeling the emptiness of the world without them. I lived in my grief bubble for a long time. There were times it felt as heavy as that knight's helmet I wore in England, a metal shield between me and humanity. Sometimes I still find myself slipping back into that space. I now see this is normal. I wasn't a bad friend, a bad mother, a bad pastor. I wasn't going crazy. I was grieving.

For those of us who love someone who is grieving and want to help, giving them grace for this bubble is one of the most loving things we can do. Don't be surprised to feel like your friend "checks out" on you. Try not to take it personally when they don't seem to be listening to what you're saying or seem less engaged in your life.

When you remember that your newly grieving friend is in a bubble, you can also understand that you don't need to be afraid to talk to them about the person who died. People often tell me that they don't want to bring up someone's loss to them because they are afraid of "reminding" them about it. Here is what I hope you can now see: you will never remind someone who is grieving about the death of their loved one because they have *never stopped thinking about it*. It is more than a thing they are living *with*; it is something they are living *in*, all the time. You can meet them in their bubble by acknowledging it.

I know the words can sometimes be hard to find. We can be afraid we will say the wrong thing and do more harm than good when we try to help. In her seminal grief work, *It's OK That You're Not OK: Meeting Grief and Loss in a Culture That Doesn't Understand*, Megan Devine opens by writing to grievers, "You don't need to move on from your grief. You need someone to see your grief, to acknowledge it. You need someone to hold your hands while you stand there in blinking horror, staring at the hole that was your life."

This reminds us that supporting a griever doesn't mean you need to find something to say to fix what they're going through. That's why your words can be as simple as "I am so sorry your mother died," or "I am sad with you that you lost your brother," or even "I don't know what to say. But I want you to know that I care." If you want to do the thing that most grieving people tell me they appreciate the most, you can talk to them about the one who has died. Tell them about a favorite memory of their loved one. Tell them what you loved about them. If you didn't know them, acknowledge their reality. "I know you loved them very much," or "I know they were very special to you." You can say, "Tell me about them," and listen as they talk about the person they are desperate to remember.

The grief bubble needs all kinds of room. Grievers walk around with a helmet of grief weighing heavy on their shoulders. They don't need to take it off just yet, and they certainly don't need you to suggest that they somehow step out of it. But they do need you to give their grief bubble some room.

8

ROOM TO NOT HAVE ROOM
GIVING GRIEF TIME IN YOUR SCHEDULE

Many of us are used to fitting a lot into our lives. We live in a world that prizes busy schedules and full agendas—and lots of us love it. We enjoy feeling productive and purposeful. The extra project at work, the time spent volunteering at our child's school, or the DIY furniture upgrade we're completing in the garage—these things can feel energizing and exciting. Those of us who value this kind of life often say yes to lots of extra things because there are so many activities that we enjoy and so many opportunities to contribute that we don't want to turn down.

If you're this kind of person, as I am, it can be especially frustrating to discover that grief can leave us unable to do many of the things we were once able to manage. It might startle us to realize that we will need room to *not* have room as we grieve.

About a month after Roxanne died, we held our yearly congregational meeting. These meetings are a place where people can ask questions and share concerns. I am grateful to serve in a church where this has always been done graciously. Usually, these meetings don't cause me anxiety. Normally, I can handle hard questions and be patient with the different things that people are feeling. But this day was different because I was grieving.

The church had recently started its own Facebook page (this was, after all, 2013), which we were using to share announcements and prayer requests. We still gave out paper bulletins with announcements at our service each week, and we also sent a weekly email. At this meeting, however, someone brought up that some of our seniors did not use Facebook and that using it might leave them feeling left out.

This person had only good intentions, but she didn't really understand how we were using Facebook. I explained that we didn't put anything on Facebook that wasn't also shared in multiple other ways—routes that our seniors could access. I explained that Facebook was simply one *additional* way to communicate the same information and that it was helping our younger congregants stay connected.

But this was not enough for her. She made a suggestion: "Each time you post something on Facebook, I think you need to call the people without Facebook to tell them what you posted so that they won't feel left out."

At the time, I can see how it made sense to her. And normally— *normally*—I would have been very empathetic. Not-Grieving Leanne would have tried to explain why that wouldn't work. Not-Grieving Leanne would have made some different suggestions to address her concerns. But I was not Not-Grieving Leanne. I was Grieving Leanne. And Grieving Leanne said bluntly, "I'm not willing to do that."

You could have heard a pin drop. The woman's mouth opened in surprise. That sentence might not sound that harsh, but it was out of character for me and not in keeping with our usually congenial meetings. I had basically said, "This conversation is closed." This wasn't how we normally did things at our church. This wasn't how *I* normally did things. The room seemed to collectively hold its breath as everyone waited to see if we were about to have a public argument over this issue. To be honest, I was ready for it. All I could think was, "I can't believe this woman would suggest I call twenty people individually every time I post an announcement on our Facebook page. I can't believe she would ask that of me. I simply *can't handle this!*"

In hindsight, I know this was not what she was asking. She was asking, "Can we find a way to care for our seniors?" But at the time, it was too much for me. It felt impossible. The woman mumbled something about looking at other options, and the meeting moved on.

Afterward, one of the seniors approached me, embarrassed. "I'm so sorry, Leanne," she said. "Bev never should have brought that up when you were grieving."

I remember thinking, "What does my grief have to do with this?" *Clearly* the only issue in that room was that Bev was being too demanding. Obviously *she* was the problem. What a thing to suggest! How unreasonable she was! How insensitive to my time! How dare she propose I call extra people every few days! How dare she imply I wasn't concerned about keeping our church connected! How did she not see how hard I was working to use every means necessary for communication and how much *work* they all were? Grief was not the problem here; *Bev* was.

But of course this woman, older and wiser than I was, realized something I didn't. She knew that my response had nothing to do with Bev, or Facebook, or the request at hand. She also probably knew that another person or another issue would have elicited a similar response from me.

She knew something that I still had to learn: grief needs room in your heart—and in your schedule.

It kept happening in those early days. I would get to the end of the day and discover I needed to take a nap. I would write a sermon and then have to take an hour off. I was asked to sit on teams to plan conferences or organize events, and I couldn't imagine even showing up to the planning meetings. I was asked to run a booth at our school fun fair, and I got anxious just thinking about it.

I now see how common this is. When I talk to people who are grieving, one of the first things they talk about is how little bandwidth they feel like they have. What once felt like simple things seem immense. They wonder why they can't get things done as quickly as they once did. They question why they are tired all the time. They are confused as to why watching the news feels like too much work, or reading a book feels too daunting, or even watching a Netflix series seems emotionally impossible.

I tell them to picture a glass with water in it. I ask them to imagine that their life is like this glass, which is sometimes full and sometimes less full. Typically, when they weren't grieving, their glass would be half full, maybe two-thirds full, with the normal things of life. This meant that if a drop or two were added to the glass—a new task at work, coming down with a cold, a parent who needed a drive to an appointment—there was space for it. The glass could still hold it.

But when you are grieving, your cup is always full, I tell them. Grief puts your life right at the brim, all the time. That means that even a little drop can make it overflow. Grief gives you a *constantly full glass*.

When I was grieving, my capacity shrunk. I simply couldn't manage as much as I once did. This not only included my ability to respond graciously at church business meetings; I also lost joy in things I had loved. I am extremely social, and I love hosting people at my home. Yet in the early days of grief, the idea of having people over felt incapacitating. Instead of being with a crowd, I suddenly preferred my own company.

I remember having some friends over for a barbecue in my backyard one night a few weeks after Roxanne died. I thought I could handle it. But about an hour in, I could feel myself checking out and knew I needed to escape. I went into the kitchen, bringing a few dirty dishes with me under the guise of cleaning up. I did put away the dishes, but I didn't go back outside. I sat at my kitchen table and willed my friends to leave before I had to go and see them again. I was gone so long that Dallas came inside to see what was wrong. There was nothing wrong in particular; I had just run out of room.

For months after my sister died, I didn't read a single book. This may not sound like a big deal, but I am a voracious reader. I rarely go to sleep without reading, and I always have a book I am working through. When I was grieving, the idea of emotionally investing in a novel felt like too much. Who had the energy to get to know these characters, to care about their story? Not me. My books collected dust, and my library card went unused.

I often surprised myself with what I couldn't do. Being asked to take on any type of task or to meet a friend for dinner or to remember birthdays felt like too much. I just didn't have room. The water was already at the brim. My cup couldn't hold another drop.

Plus, I was always so *tired*. I was tired after simple tasks. I was tired after half a day of work. I was tired after one phone conversation. I always wanted to nap. I was shocked at how physically tired I felt all the time, even though I was doing so much less than I normally did. I didn't realize how exhausting grieving could be.

It took me a while to realize I needed room *to not have room*.

Grief takes room in our bodies, and that means it needs room in our schedules. Shortly after Roxanne died, a friend of mine, who is also a therapist, gave me good advice. "Leanne," she said, "You may need to schedule grief time."

"Grief time?" I asked cynically. I felt like I was permanently living in "grief time," and I wasn't really interested in "scheduling" any more of it.

Grief time is time that you actually put in your calendar to allow yourself space to grieve, she explained. It doesn't mean that you necessarily plan to cry or wail all night; it means that you have the open space to do that if you need to.

I realized she was right. My life was full. There were many days that I needed space to fall apart, but I simply *didn't have time*. I didn't want to go into a meeting with puffy eyes because I had just been crying. I didn't want to go pick my kids up from school in the middle of a breakdown. Much of my life was spent keeping it together. Sometimes when I felt the grief welling up, I would push it down because I had somewhere to be. I needed time when I had nowhere else I needed to be except present with my grief.

We all need to give ourselves time to let our grief out. That can look like long nights when we can scroll through the photos or listen to sad songs or let our mind flood full of memories. Grief time can include visiting their grave or long walks through places we loved together. To get that time, it also means that we may have to say no to other requests of us. When I was asked to volunteer or sit on committees or take on new tasks, I had to learn to say, "I don't have room for that right now." If people asked why I wasn't available, I learned to say simply, "I'm grieving."

The blunt way to say it is, "Grief needs room to be selfish." This can be especially hard for people who are caregivers and accustomed to meeting others' needs. As a pastor, I was used to looking after other people. I didn't know how to let that go to make room for my grief. I have watched other caregivers struggle in the same way. But making room to be "selfish" right now does not make you a selfish person; it makes you a grieving person.

When a friend is grieving, we can remember that they need room to not have room. They need room to focus on their own needs. Giving them room looks like not putting pressure on them to do more when they say no to something. It means remembering that our grieving friends have less capacity to care for our needs. It includes not suggesting they would "feel better" if they put it out of their mind or did something to distract themselves. They don't need a distraction. They just need room to not have room.

This was the gift of the woman from my church after the congregational meeting that day. I still feel embarrassed when I think of my response to my congregant's question. I feel sad at how flippant and uncaring I must have seemed because I didn't understand the role grief was playing in my life at the time. But then I remember that dear saint of our church saying, "We shouldn't have asked you that when you were grieving." She knew that my grief needed room to not have room—and she gave it to me, a true gift of grieving grace.

9

ROOM FOR PEOPLE TO LET YOU DOWN
ACCEPTING THAT PEOPLE WILL NOT
ALWAYS BE WHAT YOU NEED

Early in my ministry, I met with a couple looking for relationship counseling. The couple was struggling but couldn't seem to put words to the tension between them. The man, Ethan, was angry and hurt by his partner, Christine. He shared little stories of frustration, small irritants here and there that added up. She was open, pleading. What was the matter? Why was he so upset all the time? What had happened to them? Eventually, we pieced it together.

A few months earlier, Ethan's father had died, and he felt that Christine had not supported him as he needed. Christine was baffled by this. She gave example after example of ways she had been there, all that she had tried to do. It took some time for us to unravel where Ethan's hurt lay. Christine and Ethan were from different cultural backgrounds. In his experience, when someone died, *everyone* who knew the family showed up at the family home and funeral home and kept vigil with the grieving family for a week. Christine, unaware of this expectation, hadn't done that. Ethan had keenly felt her absences. Christine had gone to the funeral home but "only stayed an hour." She had visited his family home but "only for one day"; where had she been the rest of the week?

As Christine realized the pain she had unknowingly caused her partner, she expressed her deep sadness that she had hurt him and asked for forgiveness. They were able to understand each other and move forward. But the feeling he carried of being let down while he was grieving caused a lot of damage in their relationship that took time and work to heal.

I have seen this dynamic a lot as I support grieving people. Relationships sometimes experience irreparable damage after a loss. I have seen families fight and loving relationships end. I have listened to people share the deep hurt they experienced because someone had not been there for them in the way they needed as they grieved. I have known many people who lost not only the person who died but also relationships with dear friends and loved ones because of conflict after a death.

Because I had seen this so often, I wanted to do everything I could to avoid these realities as I grieved. Although I experienced deep love and support in the early days of my grief, I also knew that as time went on, it would be easy for me to feel like Ethan: hurt by those who didn't show up in the way I wanted. Recognizing that, I started praying early on. "God," I said, "I have already lost so much with my sister dying. I don't want to lose more. Help me to let it go when people let me down."

Specifically, I prayed to God for open hands. I asked for help to let go of any hurt I felt, whether caused intentionally or unintentionally. I prayed for God's help to not focus on the people who didn't reach out and for open hands to let any hurt feelings go.

But even as I prayed, I struggled.

It began with my friend Emma. The year before Roxanne died, we had reconnected after a few years of not spending much time together. She had been going through a difficult breakup, and I wanted to support her, and we met several times that year to talk through her struggles. So when Roxanne was sick, I included Emma on a message thread I had started, with updates on Roxanne's health for my close friends.

I assumed she would want to support me through my hard thing, like I had supported her. But she never responded to the messages. In the weeks after Roxanne died, she did not acknowledge Roxanne's death in any way.

As more time passed, I grew irrationally furious about this. I knew Emma and I weren't especially close, but where *was* she? I had been there for her in the last year; why was she not there for me? Every time I made a social media post about my grief, I'd scroll through the comments to see if *this* time Emma would comment or acknowledge it—and she never did. Trying to give her the benefit of the doubt, I would go to Emma's page to see when she had been online last. She had posted yesterday! She had definitely been online! She had to have seen my messages and my post. Why was she ignoring me?

I concluded that Emma had just seen me as a counselor and not a friend after all. I prayed for open hands, but I had a hard time letting my disappointment go. I didn't feel up to talking to her about it, so I coped by unfollowing her to avoid seeing her in my feed. I was tired of thinking of how let down she made me feel.

Then I turned to my friend Lisa. Lisa was a much closer friend to me than Emma had been. We had been exceptionally close during university; there was a season I slept at her house every single weekend. I held her dear in my heart.

I had noticed that I hadn't heard too much from Lisa beyond an occasional comment on social media, but I chalked it up to the fact that she had small children and a newborn at home. "Open hands!" I would remind myself. I was able to let go that I hadn't heard from Lisa personally. I was fine until one day I wasn't, which was the day Lisa messaged me about something that had nothing to do with my grief.

I had shared a post expressing my displeasure about a conference that would run in Hamilton, hosted by a famous pastor who often spoke against women in ministry. A few hours later, I got a long message from Lisa expressing concern about my post. In it she reminded me that this pastor, while controversial, had good things to say and that my post might be hurtful to people who respected his teaching.

I was annoyed. I couldn't believe that Lisa had taken the time to send *this* message when she hadn't once reached out to acknowledge my grief. I wrote back to Lisa explaining all the reasons I struggled with this pastor (which turned out to be quite justified when a number of scandals were revealed a few years later), but I also shared what really bothered me. I was hurt that in the last six weeks, I had heard nothing from her personally about my sister. Just the day before, for example, I had posted the sermon that I preached about holding on to faith as I grieved. Why hadn't she written me a message about that? I had assumed that she simply didn't have time to do so. But that wasn't true. She had found time to write me a lengthy message about *a conference*. I told her how much that hurt.

Lisa wrote back immediately, and she said all the right things. She apologized profusely. I was totally right, she said. She had not been there for me as I grieved. She begged for my forgiveness. I told her I understood, that she was forgiven. But something in my heart had shifted. I unfollowed her on Facebook. I would take days to reply to the thoughtful new messages she began to send, and when I did, I would give short replies with no real engagement. Eventually Lisa stopped reaching out. After years of friendship, I let one unfortunate message wipe our connection away.

It literally took five years for me to realize I needed to repair things with Lisa, that I had been clouded by grief and had abandoned a friendship out of pain that I didn't want to acknowledge. I wrote her a long overdue message, and to her credit, she once again wrote back right away. And *she* forgave *me*, not holding it against me that I had dismissed our cherished friendship so easily. It was grace I didn't deserve, but it was grace I needed.

People will hurt us when we grieve. They will say the wrong thing at the wrong time. They will say or do nothing. They will say or do something stupid. They will sometimes make the grief even worse, which only adds to the pain that they cause.

In *Understanding Your Grief,* grief expert Alan Wolfelt talks about a "rule of thirds" when it comes to people supporting us while we grieve. It's a simple concept: one third of people, he says, will be *helpful.* One third will be *neutral*—neither helpful nor hurtful. And one third will be *hurtful.*

This can be a hard pill to swallow: that on top of our grief, we will also have to deal with the experience of being hurt by others. Yet when I read that, I felt strangely validated. I thought of people who had fallen into the "one-third hurtful" category: the woman who had told me not to say my sister was dying, Emma when she ignored my messages, old friends who had not come to the funeral home to visit. I was deeply grateful for the "one-third helpful group." But I was also struggling to make sense of the hurtful third.

I have met a lot of people who talk about that third who hurt them. I remember one woman whose thirteen-year-old daughter had died years before I knew her. Her daughter had cognitive delays, but her death was caused by an unrelated seizure. This grieving woman was deeply wounded by a card a friend had written saying that she could be grateful her beloved daughter was now "free from her pain." "Out of pain?" this bereaved mother sputtered to me. "She never *had* pain. She was the most gentle, beautiful soul. Just because she had special needs didn't mean her life wasn't wonderful!" Her friend's implication—that her child was better off dead because she had special needs—hurt deeply. Decades later, the wound from that message still felt sore.

So many things may hurt us when we are grieving. A passing comment at the funeral home. A poorly worded statement on social media. Being told that "everything happens for a reason" or that "at least they were spared suffering" or any of the other clichés that we feel invalidate our loss. Then there are the people who don't show up at all. The friends who act like we aren't grieving. The people we thought cared about us who seem to disappear after our loved one died.

And here's the thing: I've done it too. Supporting people in grief is one of my life callings, and I have blown it. A while ago, my friend

Sue shared with me that I had hurt her very much after her mother-in-law died of cancer. Although her cancer had been terminal, her death had shocked the family when she died several weeks before they had anticipated that she would.

I saw Sue one night shortly after the death of her mother-in-law at a gathering at a friend's home. We talked a long time about her loss. Sue kept saying she wanted more time with her mother-in-law, how she felt robbed of those final few weeks together.

In that moment, all I could remember were those last few weeks with Roxanne, which were filled with pain and trauma. I felt that my friend may have been spared a lot, with her mother-in-law slipping away suddenly before cancer had ravaged her body entirely. "Oh, Sue," I said, "You wouldn't have *wanted* those few weeks."

As I type it now, I can hardly believe I said that. How invalidating of her experience. How could I have possibly known what those last few weeks would have been like for her? I was projecting my own experience onto someone else, which was selfish and unhelpful.

Sue didn't say anything at the time, but later she told me how much my words had bothered her. "I was *craving* that time with her," she told me. "I felt like you didn't get it." I had wanted to help, but despite my best intentions, in that moment, I was one of her hurtful third.

This idea of "thirds" is really helpful because it puts words to a reality that every grieving person I know has experienced. I also think it is complicated. For example, most people will not be all one third or another. Someone can be in our helpful third one day and in our hurtful third the next.

Even more complicated is the fact that sometimes what they do one day is helpful, and another day *the exact same thing* is hurtful. Grief is funny like that. This is why we need to make room for the people who fall in the hurtful third. I realize how easy it is to hold on to the anger at the ways people let us down. It is easy to make the work of grief about how *they* have to do better. But we need to make room for those who don't get it exactly right—people who care for us but perhaps process things differently than we do. People who think what they are doing is helpful when it isn't.

Sometimes different cultures have different expectations and practices around grieving that will lead to differences in what we expect of others and how we respond to loss. Sometimes people will find something personally helpful that you find offensive. The "cliché" that means the world to one griever may feel like a slap in the face to another. And sometimes people just haven't been through grief yet and honestly have no idea how to respond.

I lost my sister when I was thirty-five. At the time, very few people my age had been through any significant loss. But as time went on, that changed. I was struck by how often people would say to me later, after they went through grief for the first time, "Leanne, I'm so sorry. I didn't know what you needed. I should have been there for you more."

I felt the same way when I began to grieve. Suddenly I thought of so many friends who had lost people, and how little I had done to care for them. I wrote to one friend in particular, whose sister had died a few years before me, telling her how sorry I was that I had not reached out to her more. I should have kept asking how she was doing months later, years later. I didn't realize she would need that. "You didn't know," she responded, giving me the gift of her own open hands.

Later, when I gave my friend Lisa time to talk, I discovered a couple of things. I found out that she had a crippling fear of death. She was truly scared to talk to me in the early days of my grief. I also discovered that she was in the middle of a severe postpartum depression that hadn't yet been diagnosed. None of the reasons she had failed to reach out in the way I would have liked had been about a lack of love for me. They had been about things going on with her.

It's true, of course, that sometimes people are selfish, or thoughtless, or uncaring. Sometimes people will be insensitive, and there really is little justification for their behavior. When that happens, we find a place to vent. We gripe about the weird statement they made; declare, "I can't believe they said that!"; and make space for all the things we feel about it. We learn to give space for the fact that sometimes people suck.

But when the hurt is really big, and when it's from someone we really care about, we find a way to address it. That is when we need the open hands most. When you feel strong enough, reach out to the person who let you down. Share that you needed something different. I wonder what would have happened if I had asked Lisa sooner where she was or if I had messaged her on any of my lonely nights to ask for prayer or help or support. I am certain she would have given it.

As grievers, we need to make room for forgiveness. We need to make room for empty score cards. We need to make room for open hands. It may seem unfair. Why should we have to find room for other people's inadequacies? But this room matters.

One third of people may be hurtful, but we likely don't want to lose one third of people from our lives. We don't want to lose friends, marriages, and family members on top of what we have lost already. So slowly, and gently, and often with a lot of prayer (and sometimes with help from therapists), we make room for those who let us down. We make room for relationships to be imperfect, room for people to be inadequate, room for people who say the wrong thing. We make room for them, as we hope they keep learning to make room for us.

10

ROOM FOR THE ROLLER COASTER
RIDING THE UPS AND DOWNS OF EMOTIONS

We all have ideas about how grief progresses: how long before someone should "move on," or how much crying is "normal," or what it will look like to go through the well-known "stages of grief." Many people get this idea from the famous five stages of grief, which were outlined by psychiatrist Elisabeth Kübler-Ross and which have become part of popular culture: denial, bargaining, anger, depression, and acceptance. Interestingly enough, however, Kübler-Ross did not apply these stages to people grieving the death of a loved one but to people who were dying themselves—to their experience of moving to their own deaths. While her work normalized a wide range of emotions when it comes to grieving, which is helpful, most grief counselors and experts do not focus on "stage" models of grief. Yet many of us will assume that we're only grieving "right" if we progress through grief in a predictable pattern.

I thought that grief recovery, if I were to draw it as a picture, looked like a straight diagonal line on a graph, starting really low and moving in a straight line going upward. Grief, I assumed, started in the pits, the low place, and every day got a little better. Yes, it would be really bad for a while. But little by little, you'd move up the graph until one day, you'd feel better.

This is not at all how grief works.

Grief is not a climb up a mountain toward the top. Grief is a roller coaster in a dark tunnel with no visible end in sight. Grief is Space Mountain without knowing if there is ever a chance to get off. And also the ride makes you want to puke a lot of the time.

I did not realize I was in for a roller-coaster ride. I had girded myself up for the hard days, but I was completely unprepared for the days that I didn't feel awful. Did it mean I was "better"? Just a week after Roxanne died, we had the most normal of days. Dallas and the kids and I went on a hike. We went out for lunch at one of my favorite restaurants. It was sunny and light and beautiful. I did not cry even *once*.

At the end of the day, I said to Dallas, "Could it be that I am already over it?" And I actually thought I might be! I didn't get it yet. I was on an even part on the roller coaster, a very short blip before it would dip again. Just a few days later, I would think back to saying that and shake my head. How unprepared the newly grieving me had been for what was coming.

When we are grieving, it might shock us to discover that we can feel pretty okay for a couple days and then, out of nowhere, find ourselves in a really overwhelming place. What's disorienting is that there is no way to predict when the lows will happen, no schedule to plan them out. Things do not always get better little by little after someone dies; in many ways, things can seem to get harder as we settle into the reality that they are really gone.

For me, the roller coaster got pretty low when Roxanne's deadness lingered into that spring, and summer, and fall. It dipped further and further each time I realized again: Roxanne was no longer "dying," and she had no longer "just died." She was dead, and she was staying dead.

The roller coaster took a big dip in July, about two months after Roxanne's death. I went to the dedication service for a friend's new baby, although nothing in me wanted to go. I forced myself out the front door and into the celebration, and then I sobbed all through the ceremony. I was shocked by this. I couldn't believe that things were actually getting "worse." This wasn't part of the deal! This wasn't how things should work.

But I've heard many others say they felt the same way at about that time after a death. That two- to four-month mark seems to be a common time that grief *settles in.* It's when the sympathy cards have stopped coming. It's when people have stopped asking how you are doing. Many of the tasks of the early grieving days are done. Now you have to figure out how to live without the person you love. Just when the rest of the world is ready to move on to the next thing, the reality—that they are dead, and they are staying dead—hits hard.

I've never liked roller coasters, and I hated the grief roller coaster most of all. I hadn't signed up for it. Hadn't bought a pass. Hadn't agreed to the ride. It was infuriating. And I hated the times that the roller coaster would fling me down into the abyss with no warning whatsoever: when I would be walking and see Roxanne's favorite flower, or when my kids would play with a toy she had given them, or when I would pick up the phone to call her and realize that I couldn't. Suddenly, out of nowhere, the tears would come.

Alan Wolfelt describes these experiences as "grief bursts." They are moments when your grief "bursts" out on you unexpectedly, triggered by things that may seem insignificant: hearing a song on the radio, seeing a favorite food at the grocery store, smelling a perfume. You may be fine one minute and bursting all over the place the next.

Dallas and I went out for our anniversary. We were sitting in a restaurant, and the Police song "Roxanne" came on. I suddenly started to blubber. I watched a children's movie with a touching scene between a father and his daughter at the end. I was undone. I walked into the mall one day, and a song I had heard on the radio the night Roxanne died started playing over the sound system. I had to turn around and leave. Grief bursts came again and again.

It could be a date on the calendar, the smell of a certain food, or seeing something I knew Roxanne would love. The tears would come, and I'd have to buckle up as I got back on the roller coaster of grief. There was no logic to it. The only logic was that I was grieving.

The burst I remember most came on Lucy's birthday, over a year after Roxanne died. It was a good, busy day, and I had not actually thought of Roxanne very often in the midst of all the preparations for a four-year-old's birthday party.

As I got into bed that night, Dallas said to me, "Oh, by the way, when you were out, your sister called."

And I said, "Which sister?"

Which sister. As if there was an option. As if I still had two sisters. As if Roxanne wasn't dead. For a moment, I had forgotten that I only had one sister now.

Dallas just stared at me, waiting to see if I had realized what I had said. I stood still, startled for a moment, and then I started to sob. I cried and cried and cried, cried until my head hurt and my eyes were puffy. The whole day I had felt fine, and then in one moment, the loss swept over me in a tidal wave.

We can't avoid the grief roller coaster. Sometimes you will ride along just fine, and other times you are going to dip, hard and fast. That is how it is. All we can do is make room for the ride, room for the bursting, room for the ups and downs, room for good days with the bad. The only predictable part of grief is that it is unpredictable.

If we love someone who is grieving, making space for their roller coaster can be hard. My husband once told me that the hardest part of my grieving was wondering which Leanne he would find at the end of the night. He could tell by my face when he came home exactly where I was on the roller coaster, and it could be really hard for him to keep up. He was very patient as I mourned, but the unpredictably of grief can be exhausting for someone trying to support a grieving person.

Know that there is nothing you can do to avoid the roller coaster for someone grieving. Know that your loved one is normal. They are on a ride that they won't get off for a while. It's not about you. If you say or do something that triggers emotion, don't feel guilty. It's not your fault; your loved one is on a crazy ride, and there's simply no way for you to predict what way it's turning.

The roller coaster is a ride we can't get off for a while. The best we can do is buckle up and trust that, while the ride bucks and flips us in every direction we didn't anticipate, we aren't going to fall out.

11

ROOM FOR REGRET
WHEN WE WISH THINGS WERE DIFFERENT

As the months wear on and we settle into life as grieving people, we might be amazed at how much there is to grieve. I was often startled by the sheer magnitude of things that I missed. I grieved that Roxanne's daughters no longer had a living mother. I grieved that my parents had lost their oldest daughter. I grieved for lost phone calls and visits and conversations. I grieved as I remembered past trips together, inside jokes, cherished memories. These were all things I anticipated that I would grieve when she died, the things that I missed from our lives together.

What I did not anticipate was how often I found myself grieving things that had never happened. A huge part of grieving is bemoaning things that will never be, not just things that have ended.

I remember grieving for a family reunion that we had never had. My parents' fiftieth anniversary fell six weeks after Roxanne died. For years, we had talked about the fiftieth anniversary gathering for our parents. With family spread out over the country, this would be our chance to all be together at the same time. We hadn't been able to do that for a while. The summer before, I had debated going home when Deanne was visiting, but I'd said to myself, "Well, next summer we'll all be together for the fiftieth, so I'll wait and go then." Then there wasn't a next year.

The summer after Roxanne died, I grieved for that anniversary celebration that wasn't. I grieved hard over one simple thing that I could not seem to let myself shake: the fact that we did not have a family picture of our whole family. My daughter was two when Roxanne died, and we had not all been in the same place since before she was born. There would never, ever, be a picture with every single one of us.

It may seem strange to need room to grieve things that technically don't exist, but this, too, is part of the grief process. We grieve the loss of dreams. We grieve the loss of things we had hoped for. We grieve anniversary parties that never happened, trips not taken, things not said.

A young woman grieves that her father will not be there to walk her down the aisle, even as she is nowhere near getting married or may not even be in a relationship. But still, thinking of missing that is grief. A parent grieves that their child will not grow up, grieves who they would have been, grieves the things they won't get to do: graduations unattended, birthdays not celebrated, milestones missed. A spouse grieves the retirement she won't have with her husband, the cruise they didn't go on, the carefree days she had assumed they would one day spend together.

To this day, I still feel sad whenever anyone talks about going to Florida. I hear the word "Florida," and I remember Roxanne's comment shortly before she died, about us going to Florida together as old ladies. I can picture what those trips to Florida would have been, and I feel their loss as if they were memories we shared rather than an idea that never happened. I grieve for those trips to Florida that I never had and never even knew I wanted.

With loss comes regret. It is inevitable. I regretted that we would never have that family reunion. But I also regretted that I hadn't taken a trip to Newfoundland the summer before. I thought about it all the time—"Why didn't I go home last summer? Why didn't I take advantage of every chance I had for us all to be together?" It didn't matter that I had had many rich and meaningful visits at other times, that in the year before Roxanne died, I had visited often and cherished all the times we had shared. I missed *the one visit I didn't have*. I was plagued by thoughts of what that visit could have been.

For some of us, the pain of regret is a particularly deep part of our grieving because sometimes our grief is complicated. Grief can be confusing when we lose a loved one from whom we are estranged or with whom we had a difficult relationship. I know that I am fortunate that my grief was not complicated in that way. For many, grief is complicated and made even more complicated by regrets that trail and track us down after someone dies.

A few years ago, I noticed a woman hadn't been at our church for a while, and I called to see how she was doing. At first, she was evasive, but after a few minutes, she shared that she had been going through a really hard time because her ex-husband had died a few months before. She was embarrassed at how hard his death was hitting her. "It doesn't make sense!" she said to me. "We've been divorced for two decades!"

I assured her that it *did* make sense that she was grieving. She was grieving the loss of her children's father. She was grieving for a man who had been a big part of her life. She was grieving for what the relationship had never been and for the reality that the relationship was now truly over. Slowly, she began to acknowledge that of course she had grief; it was just complicated.

Another time I led a funeral service for a woman who had died of a drug overdose. Her teenage daughter had been placed in foster care years before and had not seen her mother in many years. The girl's foster mother was supportive but confused about why her foster daughter was so upset. The girl's mother had abandoned her, and she hadn't seen her since she was a young child. I shared that her foster daughter was grieving what she never had. She was grieving the relationship she would never get to have with her mother, that she had likely hoped she would have someday. She was grieving dreams, ideas, and hopes. Her grief was real, even though it might not have made sense to others.

I remember a painful funeral for an elderly man who hadn't talked to two of his children for several years before his death. They had

had a huge falling-out over the man's new relationship with a woman they felt was not good for him. The children were still furious at their father's girlfriend, and the girlfriend was equally enraged at the children for abandoning the father. Both felt the other did not deserve to be at the funeral. I wrote a very careful eulogy, and the funeral director and I spent the morning managing who sat where to ensure that the two sides of the family didn't have to interact. The pain and anger in the room were palpable. And yet the grief was very real: these children had lost a father that they loved. His partner had lost a man she loved. Everyone was grieving, and everyone found it complicated. And they all needed room to grieve.

When grief is messy, people can find themselves wondering why they are even grieving. "But we barely talked!" they might say, or "I shouldn't be sad when they were such a jerk." They can't figure out why they are grieving the father who abused them or the friend who pushed them away. But of course there is much to grieve in those scenarios. We might grieve that we didn't have a better relationship with the person who died or that we never got to reconcile a hurt. We might grieve the pain that the person who died caused us.

Realizing our regrets is a big part of grief. Those regrets need room.

It can be hard to give ourselves this room because we are often told that regret is a bad thing. "No regrets!" is a common mantra for a modern generation that wants to embrace risk and its potential fallout. Relationships that didn't work out, career paths that stalled, or decisions that caused difficulty—the argument is that these should be embraced as bumps on the road, not regrets that will somehow hinder you from accepting the fullness of life. I get it. But I also think that striving to have "no regrets" is unrealistic. Of *course* we regret things. I regret things every day, from staying up later than I should have to eating the cheesy pizza when I knew it would make me feel sick later.

After Roxanne died, I could make a lengthy list of the things I regretted. Some days I regretted that I didn't discourage her more from doing the last treatment that ended up being so pointless. Some days I regretted that I didn't fly home sooner before she died.

You'll have your own regrets. You may regret fights that you had, or conversations you avoided, or ways that your relationship caused either of you harm. You may regret forgetting a birthday, that time you called them a mean name when you were six years old, or that you never returned the book you borrowed from them. You may regret that you didn't catch the warning signs that they were struggling before they died by suicide or that you didn't stop them from driving the night of the accident. No regrets? When you are grieving, that is simply too much to ask of yourself or anyone else. Your regrets need room. You don't have to explain them away, but you do need to *grieve* them.

Grieve that you didn't get to say goodbye. Grieve that you didn't get to reconcile after the last fight. Grieve that you didn't tell them enough how much you loved them. Grieve that they never really said that they loved you in the way you needed to hear. Grieve that their life held sadness you couldn't fix. Grieve that you will never see them grow tall, or have children, or get gray hair. Grieve for all the things that were not. Because those things, too, are part of grieving.

On the day of my parents' fiftieth anniversary, we were not all together as we had long planned. My sister was in British Columbia. My brother was on the other side of the province. I was in Hamilton. And Roxanne's body was in a cold grave in St. John's. There was no plan to get together later in the summer, as we had already traveled so much.

Still, we had to do something for the fiftieth anniversary, to acknowledge this milestone for our parents, so I called the local florist in their town and asked her to make a bouquet of golden flowers. Then I thought of what to say on the card. This got me stuck.

If I signed it from all of us, minus Roxanne's name, her absence would be glaring and hurtful. If I signed it with her name, it would also be weird, and noticeable, and inaccurate.

Regret. Regret. Regret. Why couldn't we have had the anniversary party we had dreamed about? Why had this not been our story?

Finally I settled on "From all your children, near and far."

"What do you think, Judy?" I asked the florist, who knew our family and who knew why I was agonizing over the words. "I think it works," she assured me. So that's what we did.

It was no big family reunion, not what we wanted, and a very poor replacement. Flowers over family. A card over celebration. An awkward message over heartfelt speeches.

But it worked. That was what I had to offer in the midst of my regret, and sometimes "all we've got" is good enough.

12

ROOM FOR RAGE
THE VERY NORMAL ANGRY PHASE OF GRIEF

In the fall, I got angry.

It started when I went to a retreat with women from my church. As usual, a woman named Margaret came. Margaret was eighty-eight years old, and it was amazing that she was able to continue to go away for these three-day weekends. One of the reasons the trip was so special to her was that her sister, Ethel, also attended. Ethel was ninety and lived with her children in another city. The retreat each year gave them several days together.

One day as I was heading up to the conference hall, I found myself walking behind Ethel and Margaret, who were walking arm in arm down the path toward the same building that I was. Suddenly, I felt an anger surge up in me in away I had rarely experienced before. I became consumed with rage at these two dear women. I was angry that they had each other and that my sister was dead. I was angry that Margaret got eighty-eight years with her sister and that I only got thirty-five years with mine. I was angry that they were flaunting their sisterliness all over the place, right under my nose! I remember consciously resisting the urge to shove these old ladies in the mud.

Then later that first night, we sat down for our first session, and the speaker told us that the theme of the weekend was celebration.

We were going to spend a weekend talking about *joy*! We were going to make lists of things we were thankful for!

So I got angry at the speaker too. Didn't she know I didn't feel like celebrating? How could she make so little space for people who might feel like I did? How could she simply instruct us all to *celebrate?* I felt irritated, cheated, and just plain annoyed.

I went to my room and hid away with my anger, avoiding everyone from my church and the friends who had come with me. I cuddled up with my rage and let it surge onto the pages of my journal and through the tears on my pillow. I hated everyone. I was angry the whole weekend: rage-y, over it all, and mad at the sisters and speakers and everyone who didn't have a sister who was dead.

Before I went, I had decided that I would let myself be sad that weekend. But I wasn't prepared for the way that grief can feel so much like rage.

That weekend was not the first or last time my grief made me angry. Social media made me angry, a lot. People complaining on their social media feeds about things that seemed silly to me. You had a bad meal at a restaurant? Who cares? My sister died. The weather has been bad for a few days, and you have the blahs? Whoop-de-doo! My sister *died*. You're lamenting that a celebrity you never met has passed away? Get over it. My *sister* died. Even cheerful things could bother me. You had a nice vacation with your family? You went for a wonderful run? You just got a great deal on a pair of shoes? *My sister died!*

I was angry at people who took their relationships for granted, angry when someone would complain about a sibling, or when they would avoid spending time with their brothers or sisters. I was infuriated when people described relationships that weren't reconciled. "If my sister were alive," I would think, "I would never miss the chance to talk or work things out with her." How could they be so ungrateful?

And don't get me started on how I felt when people would not wear sunscreen or hats in the sun. This would drive me to distraction, as

I thought of losing my sister to a disease that people could actually try to prevent. I arrived at a barbecue once and started chastising everyone there for not wearing hats. Would they like to know where my sister's melanoma started? That's right—her *head*. Would they like to know what the doctor said probably caused it? *One bad sunburn*. Would they like to know what it looks like to die of melanoma, I asked—*WOULD THEY?* Chagrined and giving me much grace, they all muttered, no, I was right, pulled hats from their bags, and put them on. I sat back smugly, relieved my job was done, that my anger had been worth it.

I was angry on the flight down to the Bahamas for our anniversary trip. The flight was a chartered flight, all people heading to the same sunny destination. The flight attendants handed out champagne to everyone to start their holiday. The mood was jovial, but one woman was determined to amp it up even more. "Come on everyone!" she yelled as she walked down the aisle to the bathroom. "Let's smile! We're on vacation! WOO-HOO!!!"

I shot daggers at her with my eyes, willing her to shut up. She was a terrible, selfish person, I was certain. Later, in our hotel room, breaking into the snack bar, I vented to Dallas. "I mean, I get that she's on vacation," I said between mouthfuls of potato chips, "But seriously? Just because you're on a chartered flight to the Bahamas doesn't mean that everyone on the plane is happy. Like, she has no idea what someone might be going through. I didn't need her telling me to be *happy*."

I didn't realize how unreasonable I sounded, how irrationally angry I was at a woman starting off her tropical vacation with a little delight.

I knew anger could be part of grief. I'd read the books. Still, I didn't recognize it in myself at first. For a long time, I would get angry, and I would put all the reasons for my anger on whomever had triggered my rage. *They* were insensitive. *They* had said something stupid. *They* were being difficult.

I wrote about it a lot, pouring the anger I felt I couldn't let out on others on the pages of my journal.

One day I wrote, "I am more often pissed lately. I am easily annoyed, and frustrated with life in general, but when I think about Roxanne's being *dead*, it just makes me mad."

And then another day:

> People whining get on my nerves. People who want to be looked after get on my nerves. There are just so many people who we need to care about, too many people whose needs I have to remember—that person is having surgery, that person's sister is sick, that person had a job interview. It makes me feel tired. It's not their fault—but I am tired. I don't want to have to ask so many people how they are doing. I don't want to remember and care about so many things.
>
> It was easier without my own things. I could help carry others' burdens because I had so few of my own. Now needy people annoy me. Now making something into a big deal annoys me—I feel like a hypocrite sometimes working really hard to care. I don't want any more of people's problems. I don't want to be annoyed with people. I want life to be what it was. I'm tired of putting a good face on things.

Anger has long been an emotion that I jump toward quickly. The difference was that before I was grieving, my anger fizzled quickly. Now what once might have been a quick burst of temporary annoyance turned into a full day of anger that I couldn't shake.

Not-Grieving Leanne loved people easily. Not-Grieving Leanne took joy in remembering people's needs and being there for them when they needed it most. Not-Grieving Leanne could let things go. But Grieving Leanne found that a lot harder. Grieving Leanne had a whole lot of what I now call *grief-rage*.

Grief-rage is a very normal part of grieving—as normal as the times that we collapse into tears or start weeping at a grocery store when we see our loved one's favorite cereal. Anger is a very normal grief emotion. It only makes sense. It's logical to feel mad when something as awful as someone you love dying happens to you.

It makes sense to be angry at the things that caused their death: the reckless driver who caused the accident, the doctor who missed an earlier diagnosis, the company that created unsafe working conditions.

It makes sense to be angry at people who haven't supported you, or who said something that hurt your feelings, or who have been insensitive to your grief.

It makes sense to be angry at the people living their lives like normal people, free from grief, unaware of the simple joys of their lives while you are full of heaviness.

It makes sense that in the midst of your grief, you find yourself angry at the checkout clerk who is moving too slowly, or the colleague who chews their food too loudly, or the president of the United States for the latest thing they did or didn't do.

It even makes sense to be angry at the person you lost. You might feel angry that they didn't look after themselves better. You might be angry that they caused their own death—that they drove too fast or took risks they shouldn't have. Or you might be angry that they have left you behind. All this anger needs some room.

Grieving people need room for anger, rage, righteous indignation, whatever over-the-top mad feeling they may have. If you know someone grieving, don't be taken aback when the anger comes. They are not angry at you, truly. They are angry that their loved one is dead.

Many years ago, a woman from our church lost a young grandchild to cancer. We met in the months afterward to process her loss. During much of our first time together, she shared about her frustration with a friend who had been overly demanding on the day of the funeral. They had asked too many questions of the family, and they had insisted on sitting near the front, where only family was supposed to sit.

I empathized. I felt angry along with her at the insensitivity of this person who thought they were "helping" but really seemed more concerned with being at the center of things. And then this dear woman said, "But you know Leanne, I'm not really angry at them. I'm angry that Jonathan died."

She was a very wise woman.

That is what we must remember, those of us grieving. We are angry because the one we love is *dead*. And sometimes that looks like anger at the person who cut us off in traffic. Sometimes it looks like anger at the person who forgot an anniversary. Sometimes it looks like anger at the universe. A lot of times it looks like anger at God.

And that rage comes out in lots of ways. For me, it came out at two dear ladies enjoying a weekend away. It came out at a stranger on an airplane. It came out on people who asked for my help when I felt I had so little to give them.

My rage needed room, and so does yours. You are living without your loved one. Of course you are angry. Of course you want to scream. Of course things annoy you. You're grieving.

Sometimes grief-rage can be really discouraging. We might long to stop being angry, and we might wonder if we will ever return to our "normal," less-angry selves. We might wonder if we will ever find room in our hearts to care about people again.

Five years after Roxanne died, I got the news that Ethel, Margaret's sister, had died. She lived to ninety-five and had passed peacefully away in her sleep. She had not been sick beforehand and had been able to live with her son until the day she died. In every way, it was the type of death most of us would hope for.

If this had happened closer to Roxanne's death, I would have felt jealous of that death. I would have had some long, irritated talks with God about why Roxanne had to suffer and die so young, while Ethel got to have such a long life and gentle death. And I would have resented that Margaret got nine decades to love her sister. It would have triggered all my grief-rage.

But grief-rage does not last forever. When I heard about Ethel, I quickly phoned Margaret at her house. Her son passed her the phone, telling her it was Pastor Leanne calling. She got on the line, and I could tell she was already crying: "Oh, Leanne," she said. "My *sister* died."

My heart swelled with compassion. "I heard," I told her. "Oh, Margaret, I am so sorry. That is so hard. I am so sad with you."

And I meant it.

13

ROOM FOR HARD HOLIDAYS (AND OTHER DAYS THAT SUCK)
TAKING ROOM ON THE DAYS OUR GRIEF HITS HARDEST

Christmas, I thought, wouldn't be harder than any other time. Yes, I was still grieving, but I saw no reason that the Christmas season would hurt any more than the other times did. I hadn't spent Christmas with Roxanne in a few years. As pastors living far from home, Dallas and I had discovered that Christmas was a terrible time to travel. We had to work right up until Christmas Day anyway. Everyone was always so busy, and the weather was unpredictable. Our family Christmases together now were more about the gifts we sent each other and phone and video calls. Roxanne wasn't a big part of my adult Christmases. I would miss her, but how much worse could it be than it already was?

I was so very naive.

It began even before the Christmas decorations were up in most of the stores. My son was part of a Boy Scout troop that was going to be on a float for the local Santa Claus parade. I don't like Santa Claus parades. And I don't like when Christmas things start nearly two months before Christmas. It was early November, and I was thinking nothing about Christmas and nothing more than usual about my sister who had died six months before. I was mostly annoyed that I had to watch a Santa Claus parade when it was still warm and sunny out.

Josiah got on the float with his friends, and my husband and daughter and I found a spot on the street to wait for his arrival. I was paying little attention to anything, trying not to be too irritated by the commercialism and hype of the parade. Then I heard it. Coming down the street, the Salvation Army band was playing "Jingle Bells." The sound was building cheerfully as the band grew closer. And standing on that sidewalk, on a mild early November day, trying not to think about Christmas, I realized tears were streaming down my face.

"Uh oh," I thought.

I hadn't counted on one thing that can make Christmas so very painful for the grieving. Yes, there is the longing to be with your loved one. Yes, there is the sense of loss. Yes, there is the empty chair at the table, the gift missing under the tree, the loneliness. But on top of all that, there is something nothing quite prepares you for: the nostalgia.

Or, as I started calling it in my head, the "damn" nostalgia. (Grieving Leanne found herself occasionally swearing in her head.)

The nostalgia was everywhere. Carols were painful. Every one of them reminded me of the year before when Roxanne was alive. Favorite movies were painful. They had been something I had loved when Roxanne was alive. If I heard the smallest refrain from anything from *A Charlie Brown Christmas*, I instantly burst into tears. It was an album that always used to play at Roxanne's house. *When she was alive.*

Everything about Christmas, I soon saw, triggered a sense of before and after. Unpacking tree ornaments was painful—not because we had decorated trees together but because every one of those ornaments had been purchased *when Roxanne was alive.*

On top of that, I could barely cope with the thought of Roxanne's daughters at Christmas. Roxanne loved Christmas and loved to make it special. How would they cope without her? How could Christmas still happen when she was dead? It didn't seem fair. It seemed unnatural, counter to how everything should be.

For weeks, I avoided Christmas. We didn't throw our usual Christmas parties; I just couldn't face them. I couldn't watch the movies and avoided *How the Grinch Stole Christmas* and *It's a Wonderful Life*, my favorites. One night I conceded to watching *Die Hard*, an action movie full of mindless shooting that happens to take place on Christmas Eve. That was as close to a Christmas movie as I could manage.

I had a book that Josiah was finally old enough to enjoy called *The House of Wooden Santas*, a book broken into twenty-five parts to read in the days leading up to Christmas. It tells the story of a young boy named Jessie who has moved to a new town and is now wrestling with his belief in Santa. Roxanne had read this book to her girls, and in the months after she died, as I anticipated Christmas, I planned to start the tradition in our family too. But I had never read it before that Christmas. I started to read it to Josiah, and I hated it. I hated it every day. I wanted to tell Roxanne that I hated it. Every time I looked at that book, I felt annoyed. I had looked forward to this book I had heard nothing but wonderful things about for years, and now I couldn't even call Roxanne to ask her why on earth she thought it was so great.

Christmas carols were hard. My new least favorite carol was "Have Yourself a Merry Little Christmas." It was one line that got me: "Through the years we all will be together, if the fates allow." I journaled little in the month of December, too emotional to even put words to a page, except this one two-line entry on December 23:

"Through the years we all will be together . . ."
Stupid.

My parents decided to come to our house that year, and I felt over-whelmed thinking of how to negotiate this huge transition with my parents: the first Christmas without Roxanne. I analyzed so much, worried about so many things.

I worried about what to do with an old doll of Roxanne's. Roxanne had given it to Lucy a few months before she died; it had been hers as a child. Lucy loved it and carried it around everywhere. What should I do with the doll? It might bother my mother to see it. Should I hide it and risk upsetting Lucy or leave it out and risk upsetting Mom?

I worried about what to give my parents for Christmas. I had decided a few weeks before to frame an old family photo of the four siblings that I had found for Deanne and Jason. I had also made a copy for Mom and Dad, but then I panicked. What if it just upset them? Should I just not bother?

I worried that my husband would try to give me a sentimental gift. I warned him not to. "I don't want any Roxanne-related gifts," I told him.

The truth is, I just wanted to get through Christmas. My only goal was survival. Like so many grievers before me, I looked most forward to when a holiday that I once loved would be over.

A couple of days after my parents arrived, my mom got a bad stomach bug. That night we were going out with friends for dinner, and the whole way to their house, I raged to my husband, "Are you kidding me? What is the deal? Now we are all going to get *sick*? Could this get any worse?"

It did. We had an ice storm, and our power went out. My parents had been looking forward to watching our children in our church's yearly kid's pageant a few days before Christmas. That Sunday we had one of the worst ice storms in our province's history and canceled church for only the second time since I'd been a pastor. No pageant after all. Their disappointment was palpable. I just kept mumbling, "Of course this is just how this Christmas is going to go. One crap thing after another."

We had also planned a potluck that day with some friends from church who lived close by. We inched our way over, glad to have a chance to be in a house with power and heat, since ours was out. But I had forgotten a very simple thing: these friends had a dog named Roxy. When we got in the house, I saw Mom's face when the dog was called and thought, "Oh no." About halfway through the afternoon, my mom couldn't take being out anymore. We came home earlier than planned, to a house without power. We shivered in the cold and lit candles. Another Christmas disaster.

A couple of days later, it was Christmas Eve. I had dreaded Christmas Eve for so long. Roxanne loved Christmas Eve. Each year she hosted a huge party and fish buffet for her in-laws, which she loved. I called her every Christmas Eve, heard her bustling around the kitchen, and listened to the joy in her voice as she cleaned and cooked and got ready for the party. I could not fathom that she was not home that Christmas Eve, getting ready for Christmas.

I didn't want to get out of bed. I woke up weeping, my pillow soaked with tears I hadn't remembered crying. I said to Dallas, "I can't do it. I'm not going to survive this."

I lay there for over an hour, completely inconsolable. What was the point of Christmas? Could I just go back to sleep and wake up on December 26? Did I have to suffer my way through this overwhelming holiday?

My husband tried to make space for me to talk. "What would she be doing now?" he asked me gently. "She . . . would . . . be . . . making . . . fish . . . chowder . . . " I sobbed. I could barely get the words out.

It made no sense! I had *never* gone to one of her Christmas Eve fish buffets. They were for the other side of her family. But the idea that she wasn't having one wrecked me. I did not want to move, did not want to have to face the day and the night before me.

But I had a three-year-old and a six-year-old who were excited for Christmas. And I had two parents visiting who were doing the best they could to get through the day. And I was a pastor with a Christmas Eve service to lead. Staying in bed wasn't a luxury I could take that day. I dragged myself to the bathroom and washed my puffy face, and forced myself to get dressed and out the door. I went through all the motions, hating them all.

As usual, we hosted a Blue Christmas service at our church that year. It's a service for people who are grieving during the holidays, and that year, it was on the afternoon of Christmas Eve. I had asked Dallas to lead it because I knew I couldn't manage. I sat near the back, tears soaking my face the whole time, sitting at a distance from Mom and Dad and their grief because I couldn't handle more than my own.

A woman named Michelle showed up. Michelle rarely attended our church, except on special occasions, and the attendance at the Blue Christmas service is always sparse, so her presence and her obvious distress stood out. After the service, I went over to talk to her, and she blurted out that her grandfather had died a few days before. I invited her to my office, handed her tissues, and sat down as she told me the story.

I immediately regretted it.

As she talked about the overwhelming feelings of this new grief, I felt the grief-rage well up and over my very full grief cup. "Why are you telling me this?" I wanted to yell. "Do you think I *care*?" Because, in fact, in the moment, I didn't care. I didn't care that her eighty-six-year-old grandfather had died. Did she know what I would have given for Roxanne to have had *eighty-six* years? Did she know how insignificant the loss of a grandfather seemed to me compared to losing a sister? Did she know that at that moment, a fourteen- and sixteen-year-old were facing Christmas without one heart of their house beating, that these children were growing up without their *mother*, and that she was sitting here complaining because she lost her grandfather in her *thirties*?

By inviting Michelle into my office and offering to listen, I had once again tried to do what Not-Grieving Leanne would have done. Not-Grieving Leanne would have been full of empathy for her, could have easily made room on Christmas Eve for her entirely reasonable pain. Not-Grieving Leanne absolutely believed her grief was valid and needed room. But I was grieving hard that Christmas Eve. I had barely been able to get out of bed. I still had a headache from how hard I had been crying, and I simply didn't have anything left in me to give. I had reverted to Not-Grieving Leanne's patterns when I invited her to talk. But Grieving Leanne was the only person I could be that day.

She talked and talked. Cried and sobbed. I did my job, and I listened. But heaven help me, I hated her. In that moment, grief-rage surged up, and it was the only emotion I could find.

It was unfair, and it was unkind, and it was unreasonable. Of course her grief made perfect sense and deserved compassion. Besides, *I* was the one who had invited her to talk! I could have done any number of other things instead. I could have asked Dallas to talk to her or set up a meeting for another day. I had invited her to share her sorrow, but it turns out I couldn't handle it. My own grief was too big.

For the grieving, holidays can feel like a month-long journey of salt being poured and rubbed into an open wound. Every tree. Every carol. Every ornament feels like a personal affront. A lot of us will know what it is to hate that there is no escaping Christmas. It's infuriating to not be able to walk in a store, walk in a house, or walk down the street without reminders that you're supposed to be happy. And it can feel scary. We might feel afraid that holidays like Christmas will now hurt forever. Something we previously loved—be it Christmas, or Easter, or Hanukkah, or Thanksgiving, or Kwanzaa, or a special day that you shared with your person—seems to have been stolen from us because of our grief.

I thought, during that first terrible Christmas, that what I most needed was to be allowed to skip over it. But I now see that I simply needed room. I needed room for Christmas to be hard. I needed room for it to be painful and bad and complicated and messy. Room for tears and room to stay in bed on Christmas Eve, wallowing in my grief. Room to skip the Christmas movies and turn off the Christmas music.

We all need room for the hard holidays. Some days are just *hard* for people who are grieving, and we need to give room for that. The days are different for everyone. A woman I know finds November 5 the hardest day of the year. In places like Newfoundland, there is a night called "Bonfire Night," when people have big fires together.

November 5 was the first date with her husband, and for years after, they would drive around looking at bonfires to remember that night together. Since her husband died, November 5 is hard. She needs room for that. Another friend of mine had a mom who loved Halloween. Since her mom died, she finds Halloween difficult.

We need to make room for different days to be hard for different grievers. I especially miss my sister on her birthday, but the anniversary of her death has not stood out to me as a more difficult grieving day than any other. My mom is different. Well over a year after my sister died, we were visiting and getting ready to go on a boat ride on a beautiful August day. My mom seemed easily irritated that day, snapping at seemingly small things. Frustrated, I finally asked what was up. She responded, "Don't you know what day it is?" I had no idea. "It's August *4th*," she said, annoyed. I still did not know what she meant. "Roxanne died on *May* 4th!" she told me. For her, every fourth of the month was a mini-anniversary of her daughter's death, and those days were hard for her.

Your hard day might be the first day of a new year that starts without them. It might be the day you would have gone back-to-school shopping. It might be the week you always went on your beach vacation. It might be birthdays or anniversaries. Like me, it might be Christmas. You have room and permission to find any of these things hard. Grieving room includes room for random or particular days or seasons to be difficult.

If you want to give room to someone grieving, remember how these things may be hard and make space for that. There are lots of ways to give this room. I have a cousin who brings my mom flowers on Roxanne's birthday every year. Each year on Mother's Day and Father's Day, I send cards to people who lost their mother or father that year. On the day that my sister would have turned fifty, my best friend came to watch the Oscars with me, just to keep me company.

At Christmas I try to remember every year what a grieving person who celebrates the holiday might be feeling. I remember my first Christmas as a grieving person. Although Christmas is nothing like that for me now (the parties, the carols, the movies—they came back, eventually, with joy), I can remember what the grieving may be feeling.

Two years after my sister died, I wrote a blog post called "On Behalf of the Grieving at Christmas." I wrote the post as a letter from grieving people to those they love, asking space for them to grieve at Christmas. Each Christmas I share it again, and my stats show a surge in views, always in the thousands. I watch on social media as people share the post and tag friends, saying, "This is just how I feel this year." And I remember.

Dear Friend,

I need to tell you that this Christmas feels different for me. Even though it may have been a while since my loved one died, facing Christmas without them is a new hurdle for me. Facing Christmas feels scary because I don't know what it's going to be like. I am afraid of all of the emotions that are going to come. I am afraid of ruining things for others. I'm afraid I won't get through it.

I know that you care about me and want to help me. First of all, know that there is nothing you can do to make this all better. This season is hard because I am grieving and grief takes time. But there are ways you can support me through this, and most of them are very simple. Here is what I ask of you:

Be Patient with Me
I will not always be myself. I don't know when it will happen. A song may come on the radio and you may notice that I have "checked out" as I step back into my memories. I may see an ornament and it will make me cry. I may see you with your mother, or sister, or father, or child, and that may be painful for me. Give me time and patience. I know I won't be as fun this Christmas. I hope you can understand.

Don't Be Offended
Don't be offended if I say "no" to things. I may be ready to go to your party and then feel like I'm just not up for it. It's not about you—at that moment a happy party is too much of a reminder of my sadness. I may suddenly step out of a room because I need a minute to myself. I may need to leave places early. Please don't take these things personally.

Be Sensitive to Me
Be aware of what I'm going through. Please don't send me a Christmas card with a quick message at the end saying "Hope you have an amazing Christmas!" I probably won't. Please don't talk to me about all my Christmas plans without acknowledging that I may be having a hard time. Be sensitive that this Christmas is not "just another Christmas" to me. It's different.

Remember Me
You don't have to bring it up all the time, but it will mean a lot to me when you acknowledge my loss. It doesn't have to be a lot. You can send me a note reminding me that you remember. You can tell me when you see me that you are thinking of me and realize that this Christmas might be hard. Pray for me.

Don't Give Up on Me
I know it's not always easy being my friend right now. I know living with my pain can be challenging. At Christmas, it may seem easier to avoid me in my grief. Please don't. I am doing my best, and even though I won't always be the life of the party, I still need reminders of life, and hope, and love. Keep inviting me to things. Include me. Maybe I won't feel up to it, but maybe it will be what I need most.

Someday I will figure out what it means to have a "merry" Christmas without my loved one, but this Christmas I don't know it yet. This Christmas I am grieving, and that is okay. This Christmas I need some space for my grief.

Thank you for reading, because even reading this message shows that you care.

Sincerely,
Your Friend Who Is Grieving This Christmas

Maybe you have your own version of this letter, or maybe you could write one, asking friends and family for the room you need on your own hard days. Or feel free to use this one. Maybe for your letter, you would insert Thanksgiving, or Valentine's Day, or New Year's Eve, or Hanukkah, or the day of an anniversary or a birthday. That makes perfect sense.

We can't skip these days, as much as we might want to. We just need to make room for those days to be hard. Because they will be. And that is okay. Give yourself a little room.

14

ROOM TO TALK ABOUT IT
ALLOWING ROOM TO PROCESS GRIEF

When we are grieving, we need room to talk. There is no right way to do this, no perfect confidante. Some people can talk to friends. Some people can talk to a partner. Some of us need a pastor, or a counselor, or a therapist, or a rabbi. But we all need to process what happened and tell the story of our loss.

I have always been poor at talking about my deepest feelings. I do a lot of counseling in my role as a pastor, but when it comes to opening up to others, I struggle to be vulnerable. I knew I would have to address this when my sister died. I wanted to be good at grieving, so I would learn to talk about my feelings! I figured one way to do that was to go to grief counseling. Isn't that something good grieving people do? If so, I would do it. I signed up for a counselor through my work three weeks after Roxanne died.

I now see that this was premature; I was trying to address grief like everything else in my life: get ahead of it, work hard, and stay in control. I was subconsciously trying to be a grief overachiever.

Things went badly almost from the beginning. First, it took me a while to find the office, which was located in a building with poor signage. When I finally got to what seemed to be the right place, there was no receptionist, so I just had to wait, trusting I'd ended up at the correct office. My anxiety grew as I sat and waited for fifteen minutes past when we were supposed to start, until a chipper woman finally came from behind a locked door and invited me to her office. I was already on edge.

Then I noticed her feet. She was wearing knee-high nylons, which she had inexplicably rolled in bunches around her ankles like my friends and I used to do with gym socks in the third grade. I have literally never seen an adult do this with their socks. I know this sounds terrible, but I couldn't help it—it totally distracted me. "Has she done that on purpose?" I remember thinking. "Does she *know?* Did the elastic wear out?" Later, I would argue that I should have seen this as a sign and walked out then and there. "Did I mention the rolled-down nylons?" I would ask people when I related the story. "Seriously. Rolled-down *nylons?*"

When the session finally started, the counselor began with what felt like an interrogation. "So before I begin," she said, "I need to ask how many days of work you have missed because of the situation that brought you here today."

I had no idea how to answer. I explained that my employer, the congregation I served, had given me three weeks of compassionate leave. So technically I hadn't taken time off work, as I had been managing to go into work most days since then.

She interrupted before I was finished. "Oh, that's tricky," she stated, obviously concerned. "I have to be able to say how much work you are missing on the form so your insurance will cover it."

I didn't know what to say. Was I supposed to leave? Lie and say I had taken time off work when I hadn't? Pay from my own pocket? Finally, after about ten minutes of questions about my insurance plan and how I felt my job had been impacted by "the situation that brought me here," she figured out what to put on the form. She eagerly plunked down her pen on her desk and smiled. "So," she asked, "how did your sister die?"

"Cancer."

"Oh," she replied, almost upbeat, as if she had figured out the answer to a riddle. "That can be scary for some people. Sometimes it makes them afraid that they will get cancer." Her voice turned grave as she leaned in. "Are you scared you'll get cancer? Is that why you're here?"

I was totally stunned. "Um. No . . . " I answered, and I could hear the edge in my own voice. Did she seriously just ask me if I was afraid I would die of cancer?

It went downhill from here. After learning that my family lived in Newfoundland, where I had to go for the funeral, she responded with a smile, "Oh, that must have been nice! Like a family reunion!" (No, it wasn't nice. No, it wasn't like a family reunion. It was like burying my dead sister, and it was like crap.)

After asking who I had to support me and hearing me say that I was having trouble talking to people, she said, "Sometimes when people die, it's a good time to cut out relationships that aren't good for us." (Was she suggesting I lose even more from my life?)

Thirty minutes later, I was out of there. I left feeling confused and hurt. She had been so flippant. She didn't understand me at all.

She hadn't even asked me my sister's name.

I went home and told Dallas that I had given counseling my best shot and that it wasn't for me. I would have to figure out other ways to process my feelings. The problem was I didn't know what those "other ways" might be. I had no idea how to talk about my loss. I constantly found myself clamming up when the opportunity came up to share my grief, and I didn't know how to ask for the space to talk when I needed to most.

There were countless examples. Right after I returned from the funeral, I met up with some friends to go for a walk. I longed to pour out my heart to them, but I couldn't seem to muster up the courage. Early in the walk, one friend asked me if I wanted a distraction. Without waiting for an answer, she proceeded to tell me about her new boyfriend, whom we ended up discussing for most of the walk.

It was unsettling. No, I hadn't wanted a distraction. I wanted to talk about what I was going through. I wanted to tell my friends about the night Roxanne died and process it out loud. I wanted to tell them about the funeral. I wanted to talk about my grief and nothing else.

But I didn't say any of that. I listened as my friend talked about her new relationship. I didn't say any of the things I wanted to say, and when I got home, I thought to myself, "I'm broken." I knew they would have listened if I had just started to share, but I hadn't been able to bring myself to do it.

Another time I was with a group of women from my church during a time of prayer. We went around the circle and took prayer requests. When it got to me, I felt too full of loss to get into all my emotions. I asked them to pray for "the expected." Surely they would know what that meant, right?

But they didn't. With genuine concern, a friend asked, "What would that be?" I was totally baffled. How could she have forgotten that my sister died only five months earlier? How could she not know *exactly* what I was thinking?

But I couldn't say any of that. I couldn't bring myself to say, "My grief is so heavy, and I need help." Instead, I mumbled something about still grieving with little explanation, eager for the focus to move to someone else.

When people would ask me how I was doing, my standard answer was "I'm hanging in there. Thanks for asking." Often I would walk away and think, Why did I just say that? I was not "hanging in." I was falling apart. Why couldn't I say what I was really feeling?

The only person I seemed really able to be honest with was my husband. With Dallas, I would let the tears flow. I could fall apart and share the deepest part of my grief. But I also knew that he couldn't manage all that I needed him to carry.

Months passed before I could admit it: I *needed* to talk to someone. I needed to process my grief in a real way. But what could I do? The last counseling experience had been a debacle, and I couldn't face the same thing happening again.

Dallas was determined to help me. He asked around and found a counselor named Christina, who came highly recommended. He promised me that she would be different. For a long time, I kept arguing. "Counseling doesn't work for me," I would say. "I'm just no good at talking about this."

But he wouldn't let me give up. "Maybe just try one more time," he would encourage me. Finally I gave in. "Okay," I said, "I'll go *one* time, but if it's anything like last time, that's it." Dallas agreed to my terms. He would stop talking about counseling with me if she told me I needed to take more time off work to qualify for her services or if she compared funerals to family reunions.

I went to Christina's office, which was in the basement of a funeral home twenty minutes away. I checked her socks, which were normal. She offered me some tea. We sat down in cozy chairs, facing each other. She smiled. She looked me in the eyes. She leaned in and said gently, "Tell me about your sister."

I talked for two hours.

I didn't realize until I was done with what was supposed to be my one-hour session that I had nearly doubled my time. When I was finished, Christina asked if I wanted to come back again. I nodded. "I'm just going to put you down for an hour and a half next time," she said.

And so I went back, and I *talked*. And talked. And talked. For me, this person was safe. As a pastor, I am a professional caregiver, and although there were grief groups at my church and many people who loved me, *this* was the space where I could receive care. And it proved I did indeed need to talk—and that I could do it, when the circumstances worked.

I remember sobbing to Christina one day, asking if life would ever feel normal again. She took out a blank piece of paper and sketched a picture. She drew a little stick person and a big circle around them. She said, "This circle is your grief, and right now, you are right in the middle of it." ("Hey! How does she know about my grief bubble?" I wondered.) Then she drew a second picture. This time the stick person was standing next to a circle. "But one day," she said, "your grief will be more like this. It doesn't go away, but you won't feel consumed by it all the time." That made a lot of sense.

We talked about how Roxanne died. We talked about my favorite memories and the things that I missed. We talked about how I could set boundaries in my life while I grieved. We talked about the people who had hurt my feelings. We talked about my grief-rage.

And one day, we talked about the tumors. We talked about this thing I had never found the words to discuss. Not to Dallas. Not to anyone. In all the months since Roxanne died, I had never once told anyone in my life about the tumors. It was a wound I could not bring up, too painful to name and speak out loud, until one day, I did.

"My sister had these tumors," I told Christina that day, trying to sound nonchalant. It was almost a year after my sister died, months after we had started meeting.

"Tell me about them," she said.

I talked about the tumors. I told her about the giant tumor on her leg: red, swollen, the size of an orange. I described the tumors on her head, her face, the ones she called horns. I told her about the wincing.

I confessed that that image haunted me at night, how sometimes I would be lying in bed, and I would remember my beautiful sister ravaged by cancer, skin and bones and bald from treatments, lying in a hospice bed with a too-colorful quilt, spaced out on morphine and wincing each time she turned. I described how she would move and touch her head or reach down to her leg. I shared how witnessing that suffering was the most painful experience of my life. How her wincing dug at me, clung to me, how I couldn't erase the image from my mind.

I had never been able to talk about the wince before that day. It was the big scary thing that had been too hard to process. But that day, I said everything I'd hidden for months, and Christina listened. I talked and I talked, and I cried and I cried.

When I got home from counseling that day, exhausted, my husband asked, as he always did, how it went. I smiled. "It was good."

When we are grieving, we need space to name all that we are feeling. To do that, we may need to acknowledge the lies that we have been telling ourselves about talking to others. I know there were several lies that I believed, ones that kept me from making the room I needed to talk.

LIE ONE: I HAVE NO ONE TO TALK TO

It is true that not everyone can be what we need. Sometimes we will talk to people that will hurt us. Sometimes people just aren't good at talking about this with us. Sometimes we are not comfortable with certain people. Not everyone will want to hear us talk about our grief.

But we don't need *everyone*. We just need a few people, or even one person. When people say they need to talk about their grief, I encourage them to find their "safe people." This is the term I use for the people with whom you can be honest about your feelings. They are the people that, even years after your loss, will be okay with hearing you say, "I'm having a hard day." You don't need a lot of these people, but it is good to know who they are. They are the people who will listen, and I promise they are out there. Don't believe the lie that there is no one to talk to—that is absolutely not true. You may have to think out of the box. You may even have to pay a professional. But you *can* find people who will let you talk. Don't give up until you find them.

For me, it was not just my counselor. I also had my husband. My best friend was wonderful. And I also had two women at church who had been through grief with whom I could be honest. One of them was a woman whose child had died many years before. Every time she asked me how I was, I would tell her the truth, and I would ask her questions. "Is it normal I'm still so sad?" I would say, or "Does it get better?" She was a safe person. They're out there, sometimes in unlikely places.

LIE TWO: IT'S TOO LATE

It is never too late to process your grief. I struggled to realize this, even though I have had people come to talk with me about grief *years* after they lost someone, and I never judged them for it. In the January after Roxanne died, I wrote in my journal:

I want it to be safe to talk about my loss again. I want to acknowledge anniversaries and not fear people are thinking, "Isn't she over that yet?" I would like to be able to talk about how often the wave can surge again and make me feel like I'm drowning.

I'd like to go back to last spring and tell that Leanne to DEMAND to be heard! To set up different dynamics. To sit with my friends and say, "We will talk about this now."

I would like to tell her that months later she'd be ready but it would feel too late—that it would still be the biggest thing you think about ALL the time, the thing that is shaping your whole life and you will feel alone in it if you don't invite people in NOW.

In that journal entry is evidence that I was believing a lie. I thought that because a few months had passed, I had somehow "missed the window" to talk about my grief. I figured that people were no longer interested in supporting me. While it's true that people were less aware of my grief by the time I wrote that entry, it wasn't too late.

The reality is that in the days and weeks right after Roxanne's death, I wasn't even ready to talk. I was reeling from all that had happened and mostly in shock. Sometimes I read beautiful, elegant things people write online in the early days of grief, and I think, "How did they do that?" I had no words for anything. I was so deep in the bubble I couldn't articulate any feelings well.

When I was ready to talk, months later, I feared that I would get on people's nerves. I was afraid people would think there was something wrong with me. I was worried I had "used up" my grief support already, and it was all tapped out. But it wasn't true. *It is never too late to talk about your grief.* The challenge might simply be learning to ask for the space to talk about it.

People *will* forget that you are grieving. It is not their fault. People cannot live with that level of pain all around them all the time.

That's why when we grieve, we need to practice asking for the room we need. We can start by saying, "I'm having a hard grief day. Can we talk?"

We can also let people know what helps us. In one grief support program, people are invited to write a letter to people close to them explaining their grief and what they need. The letter might say, for example, that they really like it when people phone them. Or it might say that they prefer when people text. It might say the dates of anniversaries that they would like their friends to remember.

I think these letters are brilliant. I have since received them as people in our church have done the course, and they are so helpful. Reading those letters, I get to see what people need, and I learn how to be there for them. Maybe you won't write an official letter, but the practice of letting people know what you need as you grieve is part of how we begin to move forward.

Eventually, I got better at sharing with friends and loved ones besides Christina. It took me a little practice. It took understanding that I needed room to talk and that sometimes I wouldn't get that room unless I asked for it—not because people didn't want to give it to me but because they hadn't realized I needed it.

If you are supporting a grieving friend, one of the greatest gifts you can give is the room to talk about it. These times meant so much to me. A couple of weeks after Roxanne died, a friend asked if she could take me out for coffee. "I just want to listen to you," she said. She drove from another city to meet me at a local coffee shop, and she made space for my grief. She let me tell the story of what happened. She gave me grieving room. A few months later, another woman asked me out for coffee. She had lost her brother a few years before, when he was in his early twenties. She explained that she remembered what it was like a few months after the death and how much she needed to talk. As I went on and on about Roxanne and how hard it was to lose her, she didn't say, "Yeah, I know right? Because my *only* brother died at *half* the age of your sister!" She listened. She gave my grief room, which looked like giving me room to talk.

Sometimes people struggle with how to give this room to talk to those they love. One thing I recommend is the advice that Susan P. Halpern gives in her insightful book, *The Etiquette of Illness*. Throughout the book, she suggests a variety of open-ended questions to consider asking a sick, grieving, or dying friend instead of "How are you?" My favorite is: "Would you like me to ask how you are doing?"

I have found this question life changing. It gives people a chance to say, "No, I don't have room for this right now" while at the same time making space for them to talk if they want to. Either way, you have sent the message that there is room for their grief in your life, whether they take it at that moment or not.

When you reach out to people you truly want to support, it's also helpful to offer specific suggestions. Instead of saying, "If you ever want to talk, let me know," you could say, "I'd like to take you out for coffee this week, and if you want to talk, you can." It can take the pressure off the person who is grieving to have the time offered to them instead of having to take the initiative themselves to set up a time to connect.

I also encourage grief supporters to take their calendar and mark a date two or three months after someone has died. This is when their friend's grief is going to hit them hard. It's when the cards and the messages have slowed or stopped, but it's also often when they're just getting ready to start to process their loss. When you get to that date, reach out to your friend and ask to meet with them. When you do, tell them you would love to listen to them talk if they want to. Instead of asking, "How are you?" try saying, "Tell me what your grief looks like right now," or "Tell me what you are missing about your loved one," or "What's been hardest the last little while?" These are good conversation openers for someone who is grieving. It gives them room to talk about their grief in practical ways.

Sometimes I think of the room where I met my counselor Christina. It was always freezing cold. The steps leading down to her office were narrow and often icy in those winter months. The building was out of the way for me, a twenty-minute drive on the other side of town. And yet it was the room I needed. It was the literal room where I found space to talk and the room where my healing began.

Now I see that such rooms—which offer space to talk, and process, and cry—can be in a lot of imperfect places. And I have started looking for them.

15

ROOM FOR LAMENT
NAMING THE SORROW

When I was growing up, there was one topic I knew to avoid in my house: my uncle Cyril. I never met him, as he had died tragically over a decade before I was born. He and a friend were out fishing on a hot July day, and they decided to go for a swim. My uncle Cyril and his buddy gleefully dove into the water, splashing in the summer sun. And then Cyril simply never came back up. They never found his body.

When Uncle Cyril's name came up in conversation, a cloud would come over my mother. Uncle Cyril was the Very Sad Thing that had happened to my family. I would sometimes ask cautious questions about him, eager to know more about this mysterious lost brother. Mom would give a few short answers before inevitably changing the subject.

A few weeks after my sister died, I was reflecting on a story from the Bible about three siblings named Mary, Martha, and Lazarus. For the first time, I realized that it is a story of grief. It tells us that Lazarus, beloved brother of Mary and Martha and good friend of Jesus, had died after a time of illness. The sisters had sent an urgent message to Jesus while Lazarus was sick, pleading with him to come and help, but the story tells us that Jesus hadn't come right away. He actually waited *three* days before heading to their home. In that time, Lazarus died. This is baffling in and of itself. Jesus had the ability to heal Lazarus. Why didn't he come sooner?

It is only after Lazarus had died that Jesus arrived on the scene. We read that Mary didn't even come out to meet Jesus when he got to town, which would have been considered extremely rude at this time and place in history. Social etiquette demanded that hosts go to meet guests as they arrive in the town, even if you were the ones who had just lost the person the guest had come to mourn. Not only was Jesus a guest; he was an honored rabbi. Yet we read that while Martha went to meet Jesus, Mary stayed home.

As I reread this story, which I thought I knew so well, I empathized with Mary in a new way. I wondered if she was not so interested in seeing Jesus after he had seemingly ignored her request to come and help. Perhaps staying home was the nicest form of protest she could muster. It certainly made sense to me.

Jesus noticed her absence, however, and asked to see her. We don't know if she dragged her feet or rolled her eyes or gave an annoyed sigh when she heard he asked for her, but we know the first words she spoke when she finally showed up to greet him: "Lord, if you had been here, my brother would not have died."

Reading those words a few weeks after Roxanne died hit me hard.

I had often preached on this story, but I had always focused on what happens at the end of the passage. The story ends with Jesus going to the tomb where Lazarus had been buried (after being dead for three days) and raising him from the dead. Of course this is the part of the story people want to hear. It's an ending all of us who have grieved long for.

But in turning so quickly to Lazarus's new life, I had missed Mary's grief in the story. I had overlooked the Mary who stood before the tomb and said to Jesus, "Lord, if you had been here, my brother would not have died." The Mary who heard about Jesus coming to see them and *stayed* home. The Mary who was sad her brother was dead.

Now, I saw myself in Mary. I recognized my experience in the story of someone who wasn't ready to let Jesus off the hook right away, and I wanted to write about it for my blog. I was at my office, and I pulled out what I call my sermon Bible. It's a "fancy" Bible, one that my father had given my mother as a Christmas gift years ago that had all kinds of cross-reference options and a thick, heavy cover. Mom had given the Bible to me when I was training to be a pastor, commenting that she didn't need such an elaborate Bible and that she would like me to have it. I often use this Bible when writing sermons because it has no writing or notes in it like my other Bibles do. My mom loves books, and she does *not* like writing in them, so her old Bible is useful when I want to think about a passage with a fresh slate.

But that day I was in for a surprise. I turned the page to John 10, the story of Lazarus's death, and saw a scribble of ink in the middle of the story. I was shocked to see that my mom had written in her Bible after all! On this one page, with not a mark anywhere else in the whole Bible, my mother had underlined—in *pen*, no less—one simple statement:

"Lord, if you had been here, my brother would not have died."

I gasped. I realized I was reading the heart's cry of a grieving woman: a sister who had lost a brother, just as Mary of Bethany had. It was the lament of a woman who had wondered where God was when Cyril jumped in the water, where God was when they dragged the water for his body and didn't find it. A woman who also looked at a grave and said, "Lord, if you had been here, my brother would not have died."

A woman who, ironically, is also named Mary.

In 2019, during the church season of Lent, I did something I had never done before with my congregation. Lent is the season leading up to Easter when churches remember Jesus's journey to the cross and his death. That year I asked people to share their sad stories, giving them one parameter. I told them that they were not allowed to "tie their story up with a happy Jesus bow at the end."

People always laughed when I said this, but they knew what I meant. They had heard the way we usually tell stories in church—the

great tragedy followed with "But God is good" or "Here is how everything worked out for the best and God's glory." Christians often feel
a need to do this, and it makes sense. We want to reassure everyone
that we still have faith, that we have not abandoned ourselves to
hopelessness. So we get to the end of telling a hard thing, and we add
a cliché like "But I know the plans the Lord has for me" or "God will
never leave me or forsake me." It's our thing, and it can be good and
important. But it can also make it difficult to share our hard things
without bright-siding them at the same time. This year, I wanted to
make room for lament. Lament is naming our sadness, regret, and
pain without any addendum added to it. It is the open expression
of loss, of sorrow, of struggle. I felt our laments needed some room.

So I asked people to give stories of lament without a nice, tidy
conclusion. I told them to let their sad story stay sad for a bit. I knew
that many of the people in the congregation were feeling like their
sad stories *didn't* make sense to them yet, that they *hadn't* figured
out what God was doing. They *didn't* know what the happy ending
would be just yet or even if such an ending was coming in this lifetime at all. I didn't have any trouble finding people who wanted to
share this kind of stories, stories they had long felt had no room in
their church home.

There was a story from someone who had to retire early due to
health issues, who had recently downsized because he couldn't handle
the care of his house. He talked about giving away many of his favorite books and how sad it made him. There was a woman whose mother
had Alzheimer's, who shared the grief of slowly losing the matriarch
of her family. There was the person who lamented that they had never
married and missed being in a family, especially in a church full of
children. There was the man whose mother had died that year, carrying the regret that his plan to have his mother move from England
to live with him would now never happen. I especially remember the
week a woman shared about her chronic, often debilitating depression. She ended with tears in her eyes by saying simply, "Sometimes
I don't want to get out of bed, and it's really, really hard." Then she
just sat down as her church family sat in sacred silence.

At the end of each service that year, I invited people to write out their own laments on little pieces of paper that they would put in a basket we had placed at the front of a simple wooden cross. Week after week, the laments poured in. Later, I looked at them. Nameless pieces of paper with comments like "My broken relationship with my brother," "My divorce," and "I wish I had said I was sorry."

We all have our own forms of grief. I wasn't trying to make people sad. I was trying to make room for *lament*. Thanks to the journey of losing my sister, I had learned that lament was an often overlooked part of the life of the church and of our culture. I had come to believe we were the lesser for it.

Lament is not always welcome in our world. We don't want Mary standing at the tomb, disappointed with Jesus. We want her on the other side, declaring the hope of new life. We don't always know how to make space for people to be sad, or angry, or regretful—unless, perhaps, they are sharing those things in the past tense.

This should surprise us, as the Bible is full of lament. There is an entire book called Lamentations, and many poems of lament in the book of Psalms. Biblical scholar Walter Brueggemann labels these psalms of complaint and lament "Psalms of Disorientation," arguing that these songs are as common, and as important, in the Bible as the cheerful, hopeful psalms we more often hear read from our pulpits. He describes a lament psalm as a "painful, anguished articulation of a move into disarray and dislocation."

One such psalm is Psalm 137, which reads:

> *By the rivers of Babylon, we sat and wept*
> *When we remembered Zion.*
> *There on the poplars we hung our harps,*
> *For there our captors asked us for songs,*
> *Our tormentors demanded songs of joy.*
> *They said, "Sing us one of the songs of Zion!"*
> *How can we sing the Lord's song, while in a foreign land?*

If I forget you Jerusalem, may my right hand forget its skill.
May my tongue cling to the roof of my mouth
If I do not remember you, if I do not consider Jerusalem my
*   highest joy*
Remember Lord what the Edomites did on the day Jerusalem
*   fell*
"Tear it down," they cried, "Tear it down to its foundations!"
Daughter Babylon, doomed to destruction,
Happy is the one who repays you according to what you have
*   done to us*
Happy is the one who seizes your infants and dashes them
*   against the rocks.*

Scholars think the recorder of this psalm was writing at the same time as the author of Lamentations or at least looking back at that same season. God's people have been taken as captives to a foreign land, Babylon, and when they are told to sing one of their "old songs," they are horrified. How could they? They would rather hang up their harps! They want revenge against those who have caused them anguish!

This is a psalm of lament. It's a story that names someone's pain and suffering and that doesn't end with things coming all together. The pain sits, heavy and unfinished.

This was the type of song I needed when I was grieving. My foreign land was the land of grief, and I had never been there before. I didn't know how to sing my old happy songs. I needed sad ones. I needed space to be like the Marys—both of them—lamenting the loss of a sibling before Jesus.

We struggle to make room for lament like this. A while ago, I was part of a group of pastors doing some reflection together. We were asked to read Psalm 137, and you could sense the agitation of one of these pastors grow as we read this text. "I don't like how it ends," he said. "There's no hope." He didn't like this call to kill babies, even pondered if it should have been removed from the passage. He simply didn't know how to make space for this text that was *all* lament. Why would we be asked to read such a thing? Lament didn't fit for him.

I felt compelled to respond. "I love the ending of this psalm," I said; I love the raw anger that is there, the honesty of their pain. No, I don't love the images of dying babies. But as someone who had once irrationally wanted to push two dear old ladies in the mud, I understood that grief-rage can make you think terrible things. I explained that I thought many hurting people would love the ending of this psalm, this space for a grieving person's lament. (And spoiler alert: God's people *do* return from Babylon. There are many happy psalms about that to come still. It's just not time yet.)

A lot of us feel like that pastor, which I understand. We want to wrap things up in hope, and we don't want people to think their sadness will last forever. We want to live in the resurrection, not Good Friday.

We so easily forget that there was no resurrection without crucifixion. We do not rise again unless we first die. In the same way, I believe joy finds its place *after* lament, the honest and real naming of our pain. For this reason, we need room to be like Mary saying simply, "If you had been here, my brother—or sister, or mother, or father, or child, or friend—would not have died."

There was a lot I lamented when my sister died. I lamented that we would not grow old together, that she would not see her children become adults, that my children would barely remember her. There was no joy in those things. Those were simply sad, awful, painful things. I didn't need to fix them, sugarcoat them, or tack on a cheerful disclaimer when I mentioned them. I needed to *lament* them.

Space for honest lament matters. Space to name the pain without having to apologize or acknowledge that things will get better. Space for these things is a gift. We need to give others this room to lament, as people and as churches.

Author Anne Lamott often writes about the loss of her best friend, Pammy, who died of cancer in her thirties. Pammy and Anne had grown up playing tennis together. In her book *Traveling Mercies*, Lamott describes what it was like in the weeks after Pammy's death:

"I had blisters on the palm of one hand from hitting the bed with my tennis racket, bellowing in pain and anger." I appreciate this image of a grieving woman smashing a tennis racket to pieces as she tries to reconcile her grief. It's the perfect picture of lament.

I share this story because I believe we all need metaphorical tennis rackets. Grievers need to hear us say, "You don't have to be Lazarus yet. Right now you are Mary." We give grieving room when we hand the bereaved a tennis racket, with no expectation it will come back to us anything but destroyed.

God is okay with lament. I know this is true because there was space for Mary. Jesus never chastises Mary, never says, "Don't you see the big plan?" Never *tut, tut, tuts* or tells her Lazarus is in heaven, and she should be glad that he's not suffering anymore. Jesus is simply *with* her. Later, he takes her to the tomb, where new life is getting ready to happen. But first there is lament, and first, too, there must be space for lament for us.

It took me a while to appreciate the important role that lament needed to play in my own grieving. For most of my life, I had seen little lament around me, and I had to learn to make space for it.

The sidewalks of my neighborhood became my place of lament. I started walking. I would walk alone, just me and my grief. As I walked, the tears would come. I would tell God about all the heaviness of my heart. Often I would sit on one particular park bench near my house and wallow in my lament, oblivious to anything else around me.

In my counselor's office I learned to lament. I learned to say I was angry, and life was unfair, and there was nothing that could make this better because a terrible thing had happened and there was no explanation for it.

I learned to make space for lament in my life. I learned to stop apologizing for saying I felt bad. I learned to simply let it sit like a lead balloon when I said that my sister died of cancer and that grieving for that sucked. I didn't need to tell people I was "hanging in there" or "holding on to hope."

As the months and years went on, offering the space for lament became a gift I wanted to give to others.

At a retreat a couple of years after my sister died, I preached a sermon called "A Tale of Two Marys," sharing some of what I have shared here. Afterward I gave everyone a piece of paper that contained a series of sentences they could complete to help them lament. The top one said, "Lord, if you had been here, _____ would not have died." There was silence and sniffles in the room as people went through those sheets, filling in the blanks and writing their own laments. Then I gave time for people to say anything they wanted to say out loud.

Sitting near the front was a woman from our church named Linda. Linda had given birth to a stillborn child many years ago, a baby she named Melanie. She never had any more children and had since divorced the father of her child. Most people assumed Linda was childless, but I knew that she had had this great loss. She had coped most of her life by never telling people about it, only sharing that she had even had a child with people she trusted deeply. Because her loss had happened in an era when stillbirths were often downplayed, she rarely even admitted she was a mother.

On that Saturday afternoon, in a chilly conference hall surrounded by the changing September colors, I invited people to read their laments out loud. It was quiet at first, and then, to my total shock, I heard Linda's quiet voice: "Lord, if you had been here, Melanie would not have died." I could hardly believe it. I'd rarely heard her say the name she had given her daughter out loud. I could see some puzzled looks from people in our church, wondering who Linda was talking about. But I knew. I knew something life changing had just happened.

Later she told me, "Leanne, that set me free." All this time, she had just needed someone to hand her a tennis racket.

On the Easter following our Lent series full of woe, we made room again for joy. A few days before Easter Sunday, I took all the little papers with people's laments and cut them into thousands of small pieces. My vision was that they would look like confetti, although I had no idea if it would work. But I preached about hope on the other side of joy, resurrection on the other side of lament. Then I took our woes, now teeny-tiny triangles of white, made into something new. I threw them in the air. They fell in a cascade of joy around me, as the whole room cheered—a cheer that felt so much more meaningful after the weeks of sorrow we shared together.

I believe that one day, every tear will be wiped away, and there will be no sadness or death. But for now, in our pre-confetti world, we can make room for lament. To name the pain, just as it is before God. To be angry, and ruthless, and even scathing in our review of God's apparent remoteness. To say, "God where *were* you?" and "If you had been here, the one I loved would not have died."

And after—*after*—we can walk with Jesus to the tomb and make new space for resurrection. I like to think there will be confetti.

16

ROOM TO RECONSIDER
EMBRACING ROOM FOR YOUR FAITH TO CHANGE

Kyle and Alannah attended our church many years ago. Eventually, they moved to another city, shortly before finding out they were pregnant with their first child. Three weeks before their due date, their precious baby died in utero, and Alannah delivered a stillborn daughter. Since they were returning home to bury their daughter, they asked if I would do the funeral.

When it was time to meet to plan the service for their little girl, I prayed a lot about what to say. I tried to be sensitive. I got a sitter for my infant son because I didn't want to bring a baby with me to our meeting. I had purchased the children's book *I Love You Forever* to give them, explaining that the author had written the story shortly after his wife gave birth to stillborn twins. I tearfully handed Alannah the book, but she barely looked at it before laying it aside. I was prepared for lots of tears when I saw her, but she was not emotional. She was simply detached. It was as if her body had no room for tears with the weight of grief it carried.

We started to plan the service, and I asked what kind of things they wanted to say. I have been shaped ever since by Alannah's words in that conversation. "Do *not*," she said vehemently, "talk about Jesus crying with me." This brought her no comfort, she said, but everyone kept saying it. She felt like if Jesus *really* cared, that he would have been with the baby and prevented her death. She didn't want any "Jesus is sad too" stuff at the funeral.

I was shocked. This would have actually been my go-to statement. Personally, I found the idea of Jesus weeping with us to be comforting. Wasn't it good news to think of Jesus crying with us? Alannah didn't think so.

A year or so after the funeral, Kyle and Alannah told me that they had started attending a new church from an entirely different theological tradition than ours and the ones they had grown up in. After years in laid-back churches with open prayers and practical sermons, they were attending a formal church with structured written liturgy, pastors in robes, and spiritual practices that were new to them. They explained to me that they weren't upset at their past churches, but now they needed a space where God *wasn't* explained. They wanted a God they *didn't* understand. They didn't want answers or explanations for why suffering happens in the world, as they found they kept hearing in their previous congregations. They wanted to focus on the mysterious God that they *couldn't* understand. Their new church didn't try to give answers for all their theological questions—which was exactly what they needed.

Grief causes us to reconsider how we see our faith and our lives. Kyle and Alannah continue to hold a beautiful faith, but their faith was changed by their loss. Grief will do that to us. Grief changes you. It changes how you see yourself, and the world, and it changes how you see God. When my sister died, I understood in a new way why Kyle and Alannah found their understanding of God changing so much as a result of grief. When I experienced my own loss, I also faced the reality of a changing faith.

Shortly after Jesus died, two of his followers were on their way to a town called Emmaus, just outside of Jerusalem. This walk was no small thing because at this moment they were, in fact, walking away from a dream. They had hoped that Jesus was the Messiah who would save their people from Roman occupation. Instead, Jesus had died. These men would have thought everything was over, that they had misplaced their faith because the one they hoped would save them was dead. They did not yet realize that Jesus had risen again. Resigned to what they thought were misguided hopes, they left Jerusalem. But as they walked away, a man showed up and started to walk with them.

The reader knows the person walking with them was Jesus, but the men in the story do not. As they walk, Jesus asks them what they are discussing. They answer him, telling him about all that had happened, that there was a man named Jesus, that they thought he was the one to redeem Israel but that he had died. "We had *hoped*," they say to this man that they think is a stranger, "that he was the one to save Israel." They had had ideas of how salvation would come, and it sure did not look like what had happened to Jesus. The Messiah couldn't die; that wasn't how it was supposed to work.

Then Jesus responds, "Don't you see that what you thought had to happen wasn't the way it had to be?" He walks with them through the Scriptures. They start to see that their own understanding of what they thought would happen was shortsighted, that it missed something, that what had happened to Jesus may fit after all.

As they walked their road of grief, Jesus helped them reconsider how they understood their world and how they understood God.

Living through the death of a loved one and the grief afterward often changes how we understand our faith and what we believe about God. Before Roxanne's death, I also had a lot of carefully considered answers for how God worked and for how sickness and death worked. But I soon saw that many of those ways of understanding things simply didn't fit when I was faced with the reality that someone I loved, who was very good, was very sick.

Reconsidering my faith was an interesting journey as a pastor. I work with people with a wide range of understandings about God, and I believe that there is a lot of space for differences in theological understandings, especially when someone is hurting. But I soon found that there were certain theological explanations that I could no longer stomach.

Grief clichés began to bother me more than ever, especially tricky theological one-liners, such as "God only takes the best." I often wonder if people think about what they're saying when they say that; the implication is that God is so selfish that he picks out the best people to take with him. Why is God taking people who are good? Are the people still alive not worthy for God to take? Another example is "God wanted another flower for his garden." What garden? Why are the flowers made of human souls? What kind of strange garden is this, and why would we ever want to go there?

I also could no longer say that anyone with enough faith would be healed. Roxanne had a tremendous amount of faith. But Roxanne was not cured of cancer. What would I do with that information? I learned to accept that there were answers I did not have. I learned to reconsider how my statements about God might sound to other people who had suffered in a way I never had before. It became important to me to also help other people see how a theological explanation of suffering that comforts one person can distress another and to consider the weight of what we are saying in our attempt to help someone feel better.

A few months after Roxanne died, I was meeting with a student intern at our church. She wanted to talk about why people of faith were not always healed from illness. She believed that God had the power to heal anybody. I also believed this, but she had landed somewhere different than I had. She had embraced a clear, simple answer to how healing worked. "Any Christian who has enough faith and prays will be healed," she said. "If they aren't healed, it's because they did not have enough faith."

I well remembered wrestling with this idea when Roxanne got sick and how much pain that perspective had caused me. As her mentor, tasked with helping her prepare her for life as a pastor, I knew what my role was in that moment. This type of teaching could do real harm, and I needed to help her reconsider. "Can we walk this through?" I asked her. She agreed.

"Let's say someone gets cancer at age fifty," I began. "You believe God will always heal them if they have enough faith, right?" She agreed.

"What about if they get cancer at seventy or eighty?" I asked. Again, she confirmed that God would heal someone of any age if they had enough faith.

"What about if they are one hundred years old when they get cancer?" I asked.

"Yes," she answered, though she sounded a little less certain.

"So to be clear: if someone is one hundred years old and gets cancer, if they pray and have enough faith, the cancer will be cured?"

"Yes, even at one hundred years old," she said, nodding cautiously.

"Let's keep this going," I said. "What about if the person has pneumonia? Will God also heal a one-hundred-year-old person with pneumonia if they have enough faith?"

She said that yes, if someone at that age with pneumonia had enough faith, they would be healed. As I asked more questions, she affirmed her belief that anyone would be cured of any disease, at any time, if they had enough faith. But I could see that she was beginning to see that her initial statement may have been more complicated than she thought.

I tried to be as gentle as I could as I continued. "So in that case," I said, "there are only two ways that people of faith should die: something tragic—like an accident or murder—or old age. Because they should be healed of any disease with enough faith."

She nodded as I spoke. "But really," I continued, "under this reasoning, if we pray for *protection* instead of healing, a Christian should never have an accident or be murdered either." She kept nodding. "This means that with this reasoning, the only way for a truly faithful person to die would be old age."

"I guess that's what that would mean," she said, slowly processing what I just said.

"Can I ask you one more question?" I asked. Again, she agreed.

"So how old is it okay for a person to die of old age?"

"What do you mean?" she asked.

"We've established that with enough faith, a Christian will die of old age. So how old is old enough? Is it okay if they die at seventy?

Eighty? Ninety? One hundred? How old does one get to be if they have enough faith?"

There was a long silence. "I don't know," she finally answered. She had stopped being certain that she knew exactly how healing worked. She was starting to make space to reconsider. As the months went on, I watched her become a better pastor as she learned to reassess a lot of important things God was teaching her. She still held on to her beautiful faith in a God of miracles—*and* she came to accept that people of faith can die in ways that seem unfair. She also understood that she didn't always have to have an explanation for that—for herself or for others.

I believe that conversation was important. Watching the death of not just my sister but also many wonderful saints of our church through the years had firmly confirmed for me: you could have a whole lot of faith and still die, at forty, fifteen, or fifty-seven. And those of us who lose people at any age can still have a lot of "I don't knows" about their death.

I still live with a lot of my own "I don't knows" when it comes to what happened to my sister. I don't know why Roxanne was never healed in this life of her cancer. I *do* know it wasn't a lack of faith; Roxanne had a lot of it. I know it wasn't that people didn't pray enough; people prayed for Roxanne constantly, ceaselessly.

It wasn't that Roxanne didn't deserve to live; Roxanne was loved and spent her life serving others. If years of living were granted based on what people "deserved," I think she would have lived for centuries. I don't know why Roxanne died and others lived, and I have made room for that to be okay.

I have stopped trying to find the perfect answer when people ask me why someone good has died, or is dying, or is sick. The truth is that I don't know and no one else does either. I think what people need most in those moments of asking "why" is room to reconsider. They need room to find a new way to understand what is not understandable.

About a year after Roxanne died, I was sitting in my office with a woman who was at what she described as the lowest point of her life.

She had already used up the only box of tissues I had in my office and had moved on to paper towels I found in the kitchen. She was going through a breakup from someone she thought had loved her, and it had devastated her. She wasn't a Christian, but she had attended our church a few times and was "trying faith out." Now, she couldn't figure out where God was at all. "Really, Leanne," she asked, "seriously, how do you find God in the midst of all this?"

I answered her as delicately as I could. Now was really not the time for proselytizing. I told her that for me, understanding everything about God wasn't my goal. I told her that I had many questions and that even when I didn't have answers, I knew God was with me.

She looked at me, with puffy eyes and a runny nose, and practically hollered through her tears, "How can you say that?" she wailed. "Your sister *died!*" Her question wasn't an accusation or a challenge. She genuinely wanted to know how I had come to believe God was with me through the awful thing I had experienced.

It was because I took room to reconsider. I received the room that great grief gives us to think about my faith differently. I wrestled with my questions. I argued with God. I prayed. And I learned that, even with all the pain, I had not been alone. I shared that with her as best as I could. I knew she probably wouldn't see it for a while yet—her story was hers, and all our experiences are different. But I did pray with her that she would sense God in the same way I had as she now suffered her own loss.

When you are grieving, you may often ask the same question: "How can you say that?" You may ask, "How can there ever be hope again?" or "How can I ever trust God?" or simply "How can I believe there can be good in the world?" There are no easy answers to these questions, but I can say this: it is possible when we make room to reconsider.

Reconsidering can look like a lot of things. It can look like making more space to name what you do not understand. It can look like discarding some of the trite answers that no longer make sense to you. It can look like long nights wrestling with God, digging into Scripture, or trying out prayer for the very first time as you take the risk that God just might be out there somewhere. It can look like finding a different faith community, like Kyle and Alannah did, or it can look like trying a church for the first time ever.

You may find that many things that seemed to make sense to you don't make sense anymore. This is normal. You may have big questions that you need to process. You may find the answers you once had feel inadequate. That is okay. The story of the men on the road to Emmaus reminds us that there is always room to reconsider—and that Jesus is with us as we do.

Sometimes we don't see it for a while. Even as Jesus explained to those men on the road to Emmaus about how the Scriptures worked, they didn't recognize Jesus. It was only later, when they got to their house and he broke bread for them, that they saw who he was. It took a while to recognize God's presence with them as they tried to make sense of their broken dreams.

But on their grief-ridden walk to Emmaus, they had room to reconsider. They had room to discuss. They had room to ask their big questions. They had room to name their confusion and disappointment before God. And because of that room, they saw Jesus. The same thing happened to me. As I started to look back, I could see that God had also been with me in my long days of grief.

I hadn't been given answers, but I had never been forgotten.

17

ROOM FOR YOUR LOVED ONE
DISCOVERING SPACE TO NEVER FORGET

I was managing as well as I could as the months wore on after Roxanne died. I had been faithfully seeing my counselor and was learning to talk in a way I had not before. I was letting myself lament. I was reconsidering many things I thought I knew and making space for new uncertainty in my life. Grief was all around me, and I was learning I couldn't skip it, couldn't avoid it, couldn't overlook it. I was giving it a lot of room and letting that be okay.

But as the months passed and I moved in and out of shock and anger and sadness, I struggled with how Roxanne still fit in my life. I wondered how to continue to make room for her in this world where she was no longer alive but still a huge part of who I was.

I had thought often about how I would remember Roxanne when she was sick. I knew this was important to her. A few months before Roxanne died, she told me about a conversation she had with a coworker. He had told her about a special celebration his family had each year in honor of an aunt who had died many years before. He explained that on his aunt's birthday, his family always got together for a special dinner where they reminisced and shared favorite memories. Roxanne said, "Leanne, he told me, 'We have *never forgotten her.*'"

I knew what Roxanne was thinking, that she was wondering if anyone would do that for her. She was wondering if she would be remembered.

That was when I told her about my plan for "Rox-mus." I had already put some thought into this. I explained to her my vision for a special event I would hold each year on her birthday. I would invite people over for dinner, people who were new friends or who I didn't know well, because Roxanne loved making new friends and she loved having people over for dinner. I told her that I would give gifts in her honor because she loved giving presents. We would tell our new friends about Roxanne and raise a glass to her. I could tell Roxanne felt comforted by my plans. And I truly had every intention of celebrating Rox-mus, every year.

Then as that first birthday without Roxanne approached, I realized something: I couldn't do it. I couldn't invite people over. I couldn't entertain. I couldn't *celebrate*. My grief was still so heavy, and I was just so very sad.

I desperately wanted to remember Roxanne. I wanted to make room to remember her in my life—but Rox-mus, I realized, wasn't going to work for me. That left me with another question: How do I make room for Roxanne in a world where she was no longer alive?

I had been struggling with this question ever since Roxanne died. It wasn't until she died that I realized how often I talked about Roxanne. I had never noticed before how often she would come up in stories or in passing comments until it suddenly became awkward to mention her. I had been unaware of how many of my sentences started with "Roxanne says . . . " or "My sister always . . . " until it felt out of place to say them.

I wasn't prepared for people's reactions when I talked about Roxanne after she died. Sometimes people would grow quiet. Sometimes they would grow emotional. Or they did the thing I really hated: the pity face. The gentle side tilt of the head and the little noise saying, "Oh, honey. . . " Lots of grievers know about the pity face. C. S. Lewis wrote about it well:

An odd by-product of my loss is that I'm aware of being an embarrassment to everyone I meet. At work, at the club, in the street, I see people, as they approach me, trying to make up their minds whether they'll "say something about it" or not. I hate it if they do, and if they don't. Some funk it altogether. R. has been avoiding me for a week. I like best the well brought-up young men, almost boys, who walk up to me as if I were a dentist, turn very red, get it over, and then edge away to the bar as quickly as they decently can. Perhaps the bereaved ought to be isolated in special settlements like lepers.

It's so true. We can start to feel as if our grief is an embarrassment to others. We become self-conscious of our sorrow, uncertain about even mentioning our loved one anymore because of the awkwardness that follows.

A few weeks after Roxanne's death, a friend invited me to her birthday party. As a few of us were chatting, I mentioned my sister Deanne. A woman commented, "Hold on. Your sister's name is *Deanne*?"

I cannot tell you how often I have had this conversation in my life. It is always amusing to people, quite rightly, to discover how cutely my family is named. Roxanne, Deanne, and Leanne. People hear it, then they say it a few times, and then they ask, "What's your brother's name?" And when I say Jason, they say, "And Jas-*anne*!" And then I laugh, as if I've never heard that one before. It's a whole thing.

So it happened again as this woman realized that the Leanne she was talking to had a Deanne for a sister. As we laughed, a mutual friend joined in and said to the woman who had asked about the names, "Oh, you didn't know that? It's funny, right? Yeah, Le *anne* and De *anne* and . . . "

She stopped.

She waited. She hesitated.

And then she said, awkwardly, trying to keep her voice light, "Yeah, it's just so funny."

And I sat there, feeling like I had been punched in the gut. Why hadn't she said *Roxanne?* She was trying to protect me, trying not to make me sad by callously throwing Roxanne's name into a sentence when I may not have been prepared for her to do so. But I felt like a piece of myself had suddenly been stolen. Had I lost this too? Had I lost this joke, this special thing? Who *was* I if I wasn't one of Roxanne, Deanne, and Leanne? A third of the joke was gone! Leanne and Deanne didn't even sound funny! Could I never make this joke again?

Where did Roxanne belong now that she had died? I felt like I was being told that she didn't belong anywhere. She only belonged in my journals or the occasional sermon illustration—in examples of my grief well planned and delivered. She no longer belonged in regular conversation, in day-to-day stories, in spaces not set safely aside for her.

The problem was that I needed room to still have her in my life *all the time.* I missed being able to talk about her. I needed it to be okay to mention her, make old jokes, say her name.

I'm not alone in needing to keep my loved one close, even after they died. In 1996, Dennis Klass, Phyllis Silverman, and Steve Nickman developed what they called the "continuing bonds" theory of grief. Their work questioned the grieving models that suggested that grief progresses in a linear fashion through various stages to a place of acceptance. These "stage" models of grieving often implied that it was the griever's task to move to places of less connection to the one they lost and that continued inclusion of their loved one in their lives was unhealthy or even pathological. The continuing bonds theory pushes back on this paradigm, instead arguing that it is normal for the bereaved to maintain their bond with the deceased. It argues that a relationship doesn't die simply because one person in a relationship does and encourages grievers to find ways to keep their loved one in their lives after their death.

Continuing bonds matter. This is why, for example, I tell people to never be afraid to bring up the person who has died to someone who is grieving. Most grievers are grateful that you are remembering the one they lost. They need room for their loved one to still be present, for their influence to never be forgotten. They need room for the bond they have with the person who died to continue.

I'm reminded of this every year when I lead our Blue Christmas service. As people come in, I invite them to write down the names of their loved ones on a slip of paper. During the service, I read each piece of paper out loud. Every year when I do this, I look out at a group of nodding faces. Yes, they seem to be saying, please say my person's name. Please remember them for me. Please make room for them. People often comment that hearing their loved one's name was the most meaningful part of the service for them. And I learn all over how much room we need for the one we lost.

On that first birthday, I didn't throw a Rox-mus party. Instead, I went to a store the day before and bought a new shirt. I know it sounds silly, but I used that time to remember her. I thought of how she would say, "Go buy yourself something nice!" I thought of how she loved to find things to make people smile, so I bought something that brought a smile to my face. My new top was blue, flowy, and very pretty. I knew she would have loved it.

Now we go out for Mexican food on Roxanne's birthday. I don't invite new friends—that is still too much. I still find Roxanne's birthday a hard day. But my kids know that Aunt Roxanne's birthday is when we go to a restaurant and eat enchiladas. We go because Roxanne liked Mexican food. Sometimes I still cry in the restaurant.

We need to make room for our loved ones, but we have to find our own way to do it. You may take comfort in making space in any number of ways. Maybe you have a tradition you will keep doing in your person's honor. Maybe you will wear a special piece of jewelry. Maybe you will regularly visit their graveside. Maybe you will do a run for cancer or give donations to a charity in their memory. You may have many different ways to make room for your loved one to still be here. These ways are all important.

A few years ago, I officiated a wedding for a friend who had lost her mom to cancer just a few months before. She had agonized about whether she should move the date of her spring wedding when her mom's cancer returned the previous September, but her mom insisted that she didn't want her daughter to have a rushed hospital wedding for her sake. She wanted her to have the wedding she had planned. After her mom died in January, of course Layla wanted a way to remember her mom at her wedding. But she had to find what worked for her.

In fact, she gave me strict instructions on what she did *not* want. She did not want what she called "sneaky grief comments." She didn't want me to say her mom was "looking down on us" at the ceremony or to throw in some homage to her. I was not to mention her mom at all. Instead, she set up a corner at the reception, with a picture of her and her mom when they had gone wedding dress shopping. For her, that was enough.

Sometimes the way we remember our loved ones may change from what we thought we would do. Sometimes we think we will do things a certain way. We think we *have* to have a birthday party or we *have* to sing their favorite song at Christmas or we *have* to have the biggest grave marker at the cemetery. Sometimes our loved ones even put this pressure on us, which is not entirely fair.

That first birthday, I learned that I didn't have to do anything in the way I thought I would. There was room for me to change my mind. There was room for me to remember in the way that made the most sense for me.

As time went on, I found other ways to make room. I decided to make a turtle wall. Over the landing on the second floor of our house, there is a wall that most people don't often see. Along that wall, I have carvings of turtles. They remind me of the conversation when I said goodbye to Roxanne and she said, "I dreamt I was swimming with turtles." Turtles became a reminder to me of Roxanne being at peace. My turtle wall is my tribute to her. It is how I made room.

This was the right fit for me. People in my family had other ideas. Dallas suggested that he could make me a memorial bench in our backyard. I didn't like that idea at all. Yet I know a woman who did that exact thing in honor of a lost grandchild who finds her bench very comforting. My parents have pictures of Roxanne all over their house. I keep most of my pictures in a drawer and pull them out when I want to. We need to find our own ways.

And we need to find ways to have our loved ones continue to be a part of our lives day to day—room to talk about them and remember them and refer to them in conversation. I struggled with that a lot. I worried that I was annoying people by mentioning Roxanne too much. I worried that people would tire of hearing about her, would think that I was somehow "milking" my grief or not moving on. I was wrong.

One Sunday about a year after Roxanne died, I told a story about her in my sermon. I had been hesitant to mention her too much in my teaching in those early days. I didn't want the church to feel I was somehow exploiting my grief. In this particular sermon, I said something like, "I'm going to tell a story about Roxanne. I know I've told a few this year, and I promise it will be the last one."

After the service, a woman from our church came up to me and said, "Leanne, me and some of the ladies were talking, and we want to tell you something. Please don't ever stop talking about your sister. We just love it when you talk about her."

That was when I realized that I didn't need to apologize for this important part of my story. So I no longer do. I talk about Roxanne all the time. If people make a pity face, it is okay. If people think it's too much, so be it. I never hold back from telling a story about her if I feel led to tell it. I give Roxanne all the room I need to give her because she will never stop being a huge part of my life.

Your loved one can take all the room they need too. Remember them as you long to do. Memorialize them as you need to. Talk about them when you want to. Say their name. Show their picture. Give them *room*.

Both of you deserve it.

18

ROOM FOR RESURRECTION
STARTING TO FIND NEW LIFE AGAIN

They say that bad things come in threes. I've often heard people make this comment when awful events happen to someone. It can feel unbearable when the horrible things seem to pile up, and we want to explain them. "Bad things come in threes" can give some justification to staggering loss: when our mother dies, and then our dog passes away, and then our spouse loses their job. There's nothing wrong with us, we think; this is just life, karma, the inevitable clumping of bad things.

But when we have one catastrophe on top of another, it doesn't really help to hear that it is somehow "typical." When tragedy struck again, just a few short months after we lost Roxanne, it sure didn't help me. Two terrible things were two too many in my book, and I thought the second trauma would break all of us. I certainly didn't think that it was through further heartache that glimmers of resurrection hope would start to shine through in all our lives.

It was August 5, 2013, three months and one day since Roxanne had died, when I woke to an early morning phone call. We still had a landline, one that indicated with the ring if the call was long distance. I was groggy with sleep as I heard Deanne's voice on the other end of the line: "There's been a boating accident," she said. There were other words: Dad and the boys . . . maybe Dad had a heart attack . . . on our way to St. John's by ambulance . . .

The short version of the story was that my sister Deanne; her husband, Phil; and her two sons, Nic and Matt, had arrived in Newfoundland from British Columbia the night before for their yearly week of fishing with my dad. We had been so glad they were going to do this trip, that they were giving Mom and Dad something to look forward to in the midst of their staggering grief. Personally, I pondered how they could face returning home again. I was still wondering if I'd ever be able to do it, knowing that Roxanne wasn't there to visit anymore.

That morning, Dad's boat, containing him, Nic, and Matt, collided with another boat when my father inexplicably passed out. It was a catastrophic accident. Matt was in intensive care. Dad was in intensive care. Nic had a blood clot in his brain that was poised to kill him any second. He was being rushed to the operating room for brain surgery.

I booked a ticket for a flight home that night and spent the hours waiting for my flight in a daze. All I could think was, "You have *got* to be kidding me." This was too much. This was the straw to break all our backs. This wasn't just water overflowing the glass of grief; this was floodgates breaking. How much can one family take?

In the airport, I texted and called my family obsessively. My sister. My brother. My sister-in-law. No one answered their phones. "Nic must be dead," I said to myself, "He didn't survive the surgery. And they're waiting until I land to tell me." A few minutes before my flight, I finally got through to Jason's wife, Lana. They were all just run ragged and hadn't heard their phones. Nic had come through surgery and was now in a coma.

It was the longest flight of my life. The last hour, I was a wreck. I became completely convinced the plane was going to crash. "Bad things come in threes," I kept thinking. "This is how it goes." I had lost the safety of believing ever again that everything "would be okay." I was convinced something worse would happen. Every shake of the plane turned my stomach into knots. I was sweating, gripping the armrests, praying for God to settle my heart, to remind me that I was being irrational, that bad things didn't breed bad things, that we weren't being targeted, that this wasn't some cosmic slap in the face.

We landed, safely. I took a cab to the hospital where everyone waited, balls of nerves sitting in the family room. We were shell-shocked, stunned. Nic was now settled in the ICU, teetering between life and death. Dad and Matt were finally resting. Phil and Deanne spent the night going from bedside to bedside.

I took a cab to Roxanne's house. Where else would I stay? This was where I always stayed in St. John's. I pulled out a key I still had, used the alarm code I knew so well. The overwhelming emptiness of the house without Roxanne hit me hard. Mike and Hannah were making their way home from camp to be with us. Emily had gone to bed hours before. And Roxanne wasn't there.

Suddenly, it occurred to me: How were we going to get through this without Roxanne? Roxanne had always been our leader. She had organized the get-togethers and arranged the activities. She had planned the talent shows, the vacations, and the sleeping arrangements when we came to visit. She had driven us absolutely crazy sometimes bossing us around, but we relied on her. *She* was the one we needed to help us manage this! For months, we had all wrestled with this question: What would our family be without Roxanne? Now we were being forced to discover the answer and in what felt like the worst possible way.

For a week, we rotated. Dad. Nic. Matt. Visit Dad in his hospital room in one wing. Negotiate the visitors. Try to stay calm when everyone kept insisting that Dad *must* remember something about the accident, even a little, no? Visit Matt, who was fourteen, in the children's ICU with a lacerated kidney, a major concussion, more injuries being assessed. Talk to him, try to keep him distracted, as the severity of his injuries meant he had to stay still constantly, couldn't watch movies, couldn't read. Could only lie there, talk, ask how Nic was through his own pain. Visit Nic. Still not awake. May never wake up. May be permanently brain damaged. Help the nurses hold down his shaking sixteen-year-old, 6'2" body. Keep him from pulling out his tubes in his sleep. Go back to Dad. Tell him the boys were fine. Assure him they were being looked after. Keep talk of his grandsons away from him. Get him more morphine for his back pain. Pray. Pray. Pray.

Try to process the visitors, the gifts, the food. Run into an old friend working in the hospital one day who sees me and starts to cry. See the sorrow in her face as she says, "I can't believe your family has to go through all this." Feel the pity from her and wonder, "When did we become *that* family?"

And how can it be that Roxanne is not here? We said it so often. We needed her to be with us in this tragedy. How could she not even know this was happening?

Each night I prayed over Nic's unresponsive body, but I never felt able to pray enough. I was so angry. I was giving God the cold shoulder. I was miffed, frustrated. "God," I said, when I let myself back on speaking terms. "This is *too much*." I was annoyed because in the three months of our grief and in the months of Roxanne's dying, I had not shunned God. I was aggravated that while our family had not turned from our faith, God seemed to be causing us so much more sorrow. It felt like we deserved better. "Really?" I kept thinking, "*Really*?" Not cool, God. *Not cool.*

I was afraid. I didn't see how we could survive Nic dying, or never waking up, or waking up a changed version of himself. My mother couldn't see Nic or Matt without crying. My father, painfully recovering from a broken back, didn't even realize Nic was in a coma.

On day three, the doctor laid out the list of possible outcomes when and if Nic woke up. Brain damage. Perhaps having to live in Newfoundland for a year before he could fly home. Missing his grade twelve year, maybe never returning to school. Never playing basketball again. Not having muscle control. Not being able to speak. Not being Nic—if he woke up at all. Deanne just stood there, tears coming down her face as she nodded, as she asked next about Matt. Somehow she stayed standing up as she heard about his weeks of recovery to come as well. As she wondered, no doubt, what Matt's life would also be like if his brother never returned to us. This couldn't be happening, could it?

For five very long days, Nic was barely responsive. Then he started to awaken, slowly. No one had prepared us for what waking up after a brain injury looks like. His waking was partial, and as he slowly rose from the coma, he cried, wailed, screamed. Hours at a time. He was now out of ICU, in a step-down unit, just a few rooms down from my father. When we would visit Dad, we could hear Nic's screams. "Oh, that poor man," my father said over and over. "Yes," we would say, "That poor man." It was not yet time to tell him that the crying man was his grandson, recovering from the accident that happened as he operated the boat. How could it be real?

We knew Dad had passed out that day because the driver of the other boat saw him slumped over the wheel as they crashed. But the doctors could find no medical reason for the incident. The hospital did test after test, but everything came back clear. We were convinced that grief had played a part. Something happened in Dad's body because of the heaviness in his heart. We asked to have a psychiatrist assess him. The psychiatric doctor visited Dad and then reported to us that he was dealing with "acute unresolved grief." She didn't say grief caused Dad to pass out, but it made perfect sense to us that his body had collapsed with the weight of his loss.

Later, we would get results from heart tests saying there was "nothing wrong" with his heart. "That's not true," said Lana. "His heart is broken." Grief can cause so very many things.

Others helped carry us through. Roxanne's church organized meals for us. Every night food arrived for us in the corner of the cafeteria where we gathered. Her friends cared for us, again. They loved our family, still. Roxanne would have been so happy about that. People gave us money, endless coffee cards, food vouchers, flights. We could barely fathom it all.

And they prayed. We learned to walk quietly into my father's room in case someone was mid-prayer. There were hundreds of visitors, and all of them gathered to pray for him and our family. We got messages of lists of churches praying for us around the country, prayer meetings held on our behalf—every community in our circles was praying. I hadn't even heard the names of some of the places that stopped everything to gather to pray for us. Oh, God, they were holding us up. They were carrying our shattered hearts.

And then, amazingly, Nic woke up, fully. And he was hysterical. The injury was still healing slowly, and it left him without his usual teenage-coolness filter. "I'm going to be so popular when I get back," he said once. "My scar will be awesome," he said another day. It cracked us up. We took him on wheelchair trips around the hospital. We poked fun at his matching black eyes, asked him how the other guy looked. When he was finally allowed to see Matt, the two of them cracked jokes as Matt lay on his back and Nic slouched in his wheelchair. We realized that he was going to be fine. Matt was going to be fine. Dad was going to be fine. And, miraculously, we started to believe that we were all going to be fine.

Us three siblings were together so often—Jason, Deanne, and I. Of course, Phil was there. And Lana and Emily. Mike and Hannah came from camp, and Dallas called every day. We missed Roxanne so much. We talked about her. We talked about what we were going through. And we saw that we were doing it. We had come together. We were there for each other. Our family had changed, and a piece was missing—but somehow it was still whole.

One day, as we stood up from yet another meal someone had brought us, Deanne paused. We were returning to our tasks, deciding who would go to Nic's room, to Dad's room, to Matt's room. "You know," Deanne said. "I didn't know if our family would ever be the same when Roxanne died. I didn't know if we could ever come back together. But you were here for me. Jason canceled his vacation. You got on a plane, Leanne. You were *here*."

I knew what she meant. We discovered we could be enough for each other. We could fill the hole left by Roxanne's absence, and we could keep going. We could still be us, still be full of love, full of laughs, full of hope.

I went home after two more life-changing weeks. The day before I left, I did two things. I went to the consignment store I had been to with Roxanne back in February. The grief was heavy as I remembered that last trip to buy clothes together, but I shopped, and I bought a new top. Then I went to her grave. The gravestone had been newly added since I had left after the funeral. There was her name, etched in a gravestone. The years: 1965–2013. A simple Bible verse. The grass still had not grown over the freshly dug earth.

I talked to her for a while. I told her about my new top. And then I said, "You would have been so proud of us, Roxanne. We did it."

I slept on the flight home.

Resurrection is not always obvious right away. It's true that when Jesus rose again in the Bible, it wasn't exactly subtle. But even then, so many didn't see it at first. The first woman to see him thought he was a gardener. Others thought his body was stolen. Some thought he was a ghost, and one disciple, named Thomas, didn't believe Jesus was alive at all until he touched Jesus's body for himself. But eventually they saw Jesus for what he was: new life. Life where they thought there was only death.

The accident was when we first saw the resurrection of who we would become: new life as a family unit, new people who had been changed but had not been destroyed.

When Roxanne was dying, resurrection was not always easy for me to remember. Most days I saw nothing but death. For much of the early phases of grief, I didn't want resurrection. Death was where I was, and death was where I needed to be. I was all lament, no celebration. That was the right space for me. But eventually I began to see that there was room for resurrection in Roxanne's story and in my own.

As a pastor, I preach on resurrection a lot. I am a *big* resurrection fan. One of my favorite quotations, from Frederick Buechner, says, "The resurrection means the worst thing is never the last thing." I have shared this quote so often in sermons that people often quote it back to me, thinking the words are my own.

But you don't know it until you know it—you know? I didn't fully see how beautiful the hope of a resurrection body is until I saw those tumors on Roxanne's skin. It was not until I saw that ugliness that I truly prayed, "Let her rise, God, let her rise, with a body that is whole again."

I did not appreciate resurrection hope until I was faced with the reality of a life's end. Had the idea of all of us rising together ever meant something to me before? It had a little but even more now. Until I lived through my very own worst thing, I didn't know the truth of the idea that the resurrection means the worst thing isn't the last thing.

It took a lot of death for me to start to see resurrection. I had never really *needed* resurrection until Roxanne died. Sure, I had talked about resurrection at funerals. I had shared my hope for eternity at many funeral homes and gravesides. But it wasn't until I stood over my own sister's casket that I longed for heaven. I longed for life without death. I longed for the day that we would rise together and for Jesus to return and make it so. I still long for that day. I yearn for the time that we will be with God, together.

And it wasn't just Roxanne's resurrection I needed; I also needed my own. Likewise, it wasn't just my resurrection after my physical death that I needed; it was the resurrection God could give me *right now*. It felt like so much of me died with Roxanne on May 4, 2013. The person I was in my sister's presence died. The life we had together died. The part of me that believed everything would always work out died. Our way of being as a family died. In my time of greatest grieving, I believed these things would be dead forever. I didn't see what could ever rise from them again. I believed I would stay dead in my grief.

But God's promise of resurrection, I eventually saw, was for this life as much as for the life to come. God would bring me new life even when I couldn't see it—even when he was right in front of me, and all I thought I saw was the gardener because I didn't know what Jesus could look like yet.

For me, that resurrection started with the accident, an accident from which everyone fully recovered, much to all the doctors' surprise. We started to rise again. We became something new. There was a lot of grief still on the way, but we found out we could live. Slowly, my life rose again. After a while, I started inviting people back to our house. As the years went on, I threw Christmas parties again. Eventually, I was able to give away the clothes of Roxanne's that didn't fit me. I learned to say her name. As I made space for resurrection, more and more of it crept in.

I still do not know why our prayers to spare Nic's life were answered while our prayers to save Roxanne were not. And I have learned to make room for resurrection hope to be real in both scenarios. One resurrection will be in the life to come, and one we get to see while we are still alive. They are both beautiful.

While we were visiting Roxanne in the last days of her life, I picked up a book I had given her a few months before: *Traveling Mercies* by Anne Lamott. I smiled as I flipped through it and saw that she had underlined parts of the book. Unlike my mom, Roxanne had no trouble underlining her books, and I was so pleased she had liked it enough to do so. But then my eyes caught on one underlined sentence. It read: "I know that a basic tenet of the Christian faith is that death is really just a major change of address."

I pictured Roxanne reading those words a few months before she died, knowing her address change was close at hand. I imagined her taking the time to find a pen to underline it. I thought of her making space in her life for resurrection, acknowledging that there was new life to come for her.

In our darkest days, making room for resurrection may seem like a ridiculous suggestion, especially when the bad things keep coming. Let me assure you, you don't need to rush to resurrection. But I invite you to make some room for resurrection because while it may or may not be true that bad things come in threes, this *is* certain: the worst thing does not have to be the last thing.

19

ROOM TO NEVER GET OVER IT
ALWAYS MISSING THE ONE YOU LOST

It's true what my counselor told me: that there is a season when you live right inside that big cloud of grief. In the grief bubble, it feels like you live surrounded by grief all the time. This is a normal part of grieving. It is also true that at some point, we transition to a time where we live beside the bubble, instead of inside it. Moving to this season can take a long time. Even when the big cloud shifts, your grief never really leaves. It is still part of us, forever.

That's why you need room for your grief for the rest of your life. Even when things start shifting, and even after you move to that place where the bubble is beside you instead of all around you, your grief still needs room. This can be hard to understand because people will often focus on the idea of "getting over" our loss. Sadly, people often ask grievers some version of the question "Are you over it yet?" This can lead to the misconception that our goal is to reach a place where our grief ceases to exist.

I carried this unrealistic goal for myself. When I was in the early days of my grief, two interlocking and warring thoughts dominated my thinking and made me afraid for my future:

1. I need to get over this.
2. I'll never get over this.

These were both wrong and right.

I did need to find a way to move forward—*and* there is no "getting over" grief in the way we often define it. "Getting over" things, for most people, means that they have let something go, that they have "moved on," that they have healed and are back where they started. Grief doesn't work like that.

When we lose someone we love, we are never the same again. We are forever changed by the loss, forever transformed. In that way, we don't get over it, and we need room for that to be okay. Like so many other things, I had to learn this one too.

In 2018, a movie came out that chronicled the life of Freddie Mercury, lead singer of the rock band Queen, called *Bohemian Rhapsody*. I went to see it one afternoon with my best friend, Sharlene. As the movie opened, we found ourselves watching a scene from the now-famous fundraising concert "Live Aid" that happened in London in 1985. My heart skipped a beat. "Roxanne was there," I whispered to Sharlene, proudly.

When she was just nineteen, Roxanne spent the first of several stints living in England, working in a London shoe store to save up money to travel throughout Europe during her summer break. She told me she had gotten tickets to this concert that sounded good, but she couldn't get the time off. She thought she couldn't go, until a friend pointed out to her that it may truly be a once-in-a-lifetime opportunity. She took the risk of losing her job and called in sick—something she had never done before and probably never did again after—and thus got to go to one of the most iconic concerts in modern history. She had often told me about the moment Queen took the stage, how they had stolen the show and electrified the audience.

It was impossible not to think of Roxanne after seeing that "Live Aid" scene. As the movie went on, I thought of Roxanne more and more, growing increasingly sad that she had not lived to see this film. The movie reaches its climax with a return to the Live Aid concert. Twelve full minutes of a concert I had heard about so often. The whole time, I was thinking, "Roxanne was there" and "Roxanne would love this." Where was she standing? What else did she remember? If I looked in the audience scenes from the footage of the original concert, would I see her, just a glimpse?

My grief started to surge. The screen blurred as tears began to trickle down my cheeks. I wanted Roxanne to watch this movie. I wanted to talk to her about Live Aid. I wanted her to still be alive. She had been dead for over five years at this point, and her absence felt as gaping as it had in the first few months of losing her.

I turned to Sharlene as the movie ended. "That was a little grief-triggering for me," I spurted out, before I started completely sobbing. Sharlene sat and waited as I cried my heavy tears. After a while, she said, "It was really cool Roxanne was there." I nodded and agreed, pulled myself together, and went to the bathroom to wash my face. I looked like I had come out of the world's saddest movie rather than a rock biopic. I was a total mess, right smack in the midst of the bubble again in a movie theater bathroom.

In March 2020, Roxanne's daughter Emily came to live with us, moving in right at the start of the shutdown for the pandemic. She had just graduated from university and gotten a job in a town next to ours. She was given a lot of perks, including a company car, and one day I drove her to the lot to pick it up.

It was a ridiculous day. It was pouring rain, and it was the first time either of us had gone anywhere vaguely "public" since the lockdown had started two weeks before. Everyone was feeling panicky about COVID-19. We brought Lysol wipes to wipe down every inch of her new car before she started driving. We had gloves because she would have to touch the set of keys the dealer gave her. When she got out to talk to the attendants in the lot, I stayed in the car, avoiding any contact I could with others.

But when she got ready to step in the car, I insisted on taking a picture. "Em's first car!" I cheered through the rain as she held up the keys. She smiled big, graciously not rolling her eyes too hard. We each got in our vehicles, and I pulled out of the parking lot, looking in the rear-view mirror to make sure Emily was following.

That's when it happened. As I looked at my sister's daughter sitting in her new car, a confident, grown woman, all I could think was, "Roxanne would be so proud of her. I wish Roxanne could be here for this." And I cried all the way home, my car a bubble of grief.

There have been countless other moments. To this day, wherever I hear the song "Daylight," which played as I drove to the hospital the night Roxanne died, tears come to my eyes. Nearly a decade later, my throat catches when I sing the song "10,000 Reasons" at my church, which we sang so often the year after Roxanne died. I still cannot listen to the Charlie Brown Christmas album unless I want to be totally undone.

It surprises many people to learn that a typical "grief cycle"—the time it takes for grief to move from the space where you live inside the circle to the circle being next to you, as my counselor explained—takes at least two to four years. Frequently, I talk to people a year or two after their loss, and they feel embarrassed to still be struggling with their grief. "I should be over it by now," they say.

When I tell them that two to four years is a "typical" minimum grief cycle (and that many take even longer), they are not saddened by this. They are *relieved*. They realize that there is nothing wrong with them. Of course they are still struggling! Grief takes time. They are not "over it" yet—and in fact, getting over it is not the goal. Grief simply doesn't work that way.

Grieving people need room to remember their loved ones. They need room to be sad weeks, months, and years after a loss. And yes, many people will find their cycle of grief is far longer than two to four years. They need room to miss their people on special occasions. They need room to remember their loved one with tears and with laughter. They need it to be okay that they never truly "get over it."

I remember talking to my friend shortly after her own sister died too young. She said, "My heart is broken, and I can't imagine that it will ever heal again—because how can it fit back together when a piece of it is missing?"

She describes it so well. Our hearts meld back together with cuts and scars and jagged edges, and it is exactly true that for the rest of our lives; there will be that little piece that isn't there, a piece that belongs still to the one we lost. We will always carry the injury of our broken hearts.

As the first year of my grieving passed, and then the second, and then the third, I learned to make space for an important truth: I would always grieve Roxanne's death. It was a scar that would mark me for the rest of my life. It would always be part of who I was. It would always hurt to miss her. The idea I had that I would one day wake up and find that I had "moved on" was not how it worked. Instead, I would move forward as a new version of myself. I did not need to "get over" Roxanne's death.

But I was also wrong when I found myself thinking I would "never get over it." There were days I thought the pain would always be unbearable, that my grief would consume the rest of my life. This has also not been true. We carry our grief with us, but there will come a time that we realize we have stepped out of the bubble. It is not all around us anymore. It is a part of us, but it is not *all* of us.

For me, I saw that my friend's promise about learning to ride the wave was true. As the years went on, the waves still came. But they were farther apart. And less horrendous. And I discovered that I had learned how to surf.

My grief still sneaks up on me all the time, but there is more in my life than my grief. Still, my grief needs room. Room after a Queen movie. Room when the song comes on at the mall. Room when my beautiful nieces remind me of the amazing mother I miss with them.

Give the grieving a little room. We aren't over it *and* we are moving forward.

20

ROOM FOR REDEMPTION
CLEARING SPACE FOR GOOD TO COME FROM BAD

Redemption is a funny thing. The idea can get misused and mis-represented. It can sound like we are trying to justify horrible things, claiming that God caused something awful to bring about something good. I don't believe that, not even a little.

But I do believe that God doesn't waste our hard things. I believe they can be used to heal, to bring hope, to change us, and to help others. I believe in redemption.

About a year after Roxanne's death, I got a phone call from Dena, a former neighbor. I was surprised and delighted. Dena had lived next door to me a couple of years earlier, but we had not talked in ages. I answered the phone cheerfully, "Hi Dena! How are you?" I expected a chance to catch up or perhaps hear a story of something epic that always seemed to happen to Dena—like partying with Nicholas Cage in Las Vegas or starting a new vintage clothing store on a whim that was blowing up on Twitter.

Instead, I was met with a voice in total distress: "I'm not so good, Leanne," she said. And she told me why.

Dena was the oldest of four children, and she had two sisters and one brother, just like me. I had met her siblings lots of times, when they gathered at her house for birthday gatherings and pool parties that ended up spilling over to chats in our driveway and around our front step. The family was very close.

With shock still in her voice, Dena told me that her youngest sister, Maria, had not woken up from her sleep a few days earlier. She had apparently had a seizure in the middle of the night. And she was not going to wake up. They were getting ready to take her off life support. My heart sank. "I'm so, so sorry Dena," I told her.

She then shared that she was calling with a request. Maria was engaged to be married to a man named Ricky, the father of her one-year-old baby. He wanted to get married before they ended Maria's life support. Could I do that? Could I marry them?

I explained the legal realities. Without a license and without Maria's ability to consent to the wedding, as she was in a coma, I couldn't do a legal wedding. But, I told her, I could do a ceremony. I could come and do a wedding, with God as a witness to Ricky's pledge and Maria's desire. This, Dena said, is what they wanted. Could I come tonight? Could I do it right away?

Yes, I said, of course I could.

I got off the phone, changed into my most appropriate wedding officiant attire, and rushed out the door. On my way to the hospital, I tried to think of what they would need. I stopped at a local florist by my house and requested a boutonniere and a small corsage for the bride and groom. Could these somehow be enough? Then I drove to the parking lot in the hospital, pulled out my clergy pass, smoothed my hair . . . and suddenly I stopped.

I didn't want to do this. I did not want to walk into a hospital room where a family was getting ready to say goodbye to their sister. My own sister's death had been too recent. I didn't know if I could handle the bedside of a sister about to die. I was crying already.

But it was what I had been asked to do, called to do, something I *could* do. I took a breath. Then I took my Bible, my notes, and the last-minute flowers and walked to the intensive care unit.

I saw Dena almost immediately, hugged her hard. She asked if we could go for a walk before we started, and we found an empty hallway to pace together. Dena told me what happened the day her sister had her seizure, how impossible and awful it still felt. She told me about the little boy who was left, how he was still crying to be nursed every day, how she ached to help him and couldn't. She told me that she didn't believe her heart would ever heal.

And then she said to me, "I called you because I knew you had lost a sister. I knew you would understand."

There it was. The reality was that any of the many hospital chaplains could have done this ceremony. They had offered. But she wanted someone who would understand, someone who shared her pain. And that was me.

This, I knew, was redemption. This was something that I now had to offer the world. I was a woman who had known grief. My sister had also died.

Eventually, Dena was ready to go back to her sister's hospital room and start the ceremony. I thought it would just be a couple of family members, but the room was packed with friends and loved ones. There was barely room to stand. The room was bursting with love and trauma.

I had thought about the words of the wedding ceremony on my drive to the hospital, contemplated if some of them were too painful or unreasonable to say. But I realized that to change them would be so noticeable that it would hurt in a different way. So, I said them anyway, tears pouring down my own face—"Do you, Maria, take this man Ricky to have and to hold, until you are parted by death?"

In my whole life I have never felt something like I did in that moment. It felt like the physical rocking of a ship, as the whole room let out one big gulp of collective despair.

And on Maria's behalf, her sisters answered, "Yes."

Oh God, I thought later, thank you. Thank you that Dena believed I could understand. Thank you that when she needed someone, she called me, one broken-hearted sister reaching out to another.

Two hours later, they took Maria off life support, and she gently slipped away.

Two years later, when I ran into Dena one day, she told me that Ricky still kept the boutonniere I had purchased on his bedside table, his one memento of his wedding.

In the years that followed Roxanne's death, grief and lament have become two of my favorite topics to talk about. I preach on these concepts often, talk about them at conferences, write about them online. And I still get calls from friends who ask, "Could I talk to you? I know you will understand."

And I do. God has allowed me to use my grief to help others in my church, friends from my neighborhood, and strangers who follow me on social media. This has been my redemption, and it brings me joy.

To be clear, I don't believe that God gave my sister cancer so that I could help people through grief. I think an awful thing happened in a broken world. Terrible things happen all the time—accidents that kill children, disasters that steal lives in a blink, inexplicable illnesses we cannot fix—and I don't believe God makes them happen so that we can become better people or eventually help others when bad things happen to them. Awful things just happen. *And* good things sometimes come from them because of what we've learned or how they move us to help others in a new way.

It doesn't mean we have to be glad the bad things happened. I empathize with a scene from the movie *Calendar Girls*. In this movie, a woman loses her husband to cancer, and she and her friends decide to raise money to refurnish the family room at the local cancer unit at the hospital where he was treated in his honor. They end up deciding to create a nude calendar—featuring themselves. It's a hilarious movie as a group of senior citizens ends up raising millions for the hospital—becoming international sensations while they're at—when their goal had just been to raise enough to buy a new chesterfield.

But one day, the two main characters, fresh off the news that they have been invited to be on *The Late Show* to promote their calendar, get in an argument. The woman whose husband died doesn't want to go. "Why ever not?" her best friend asks her.

"Because I don't want it!" the widowed woman yells. "Don't you understand? I would rather him be *alive*. I would give back every cent we raised for him to be *alive*. I still want *him!*"

I totally get it. Sometimes people comment to me about my "success" as a grief educator. "Wow, you have so many followers on Instagram!" they say, or "Did you see how many hits your last post had? You're Insta-famous!" I open messages from strangers telling me my writings have helped them survive, that my page is a lifeline. I am glad. But if it somehow came down to choosing between helping people with their grief or getting to keep my sister, I would still pick Roxanne being alive. Hands down.

Making room for redemption doesn't mean that you ever have to say it is okay your loved one died. It doesn't mean that we accept that what happened was a good thing. It doesn't justify the accident, the trauma, the tragic thing. It means that we see that something new may still come, even if it is in forms we didn't imagine.

Less than a year after Roxanne died, it was time to plan another Easter service for our church. I had struggled a lot the Lenten season leading up to that Easter Sunday. All the memories of going to visit Roxanne in Newfoundland, shopping together, talking about burial clothes, writing eulogies, and watching her body whither hit me with each day of the calendar. Once again, I was left wondering what to do for Easter.

A few years before, we had boxed up a number of tattered hymnals that were no longer useable. For years, they had sat in storage, and no one knew quite what to do with them. That year, I had an idea. A few weeks before, I gathered some of the crafty folks from our congregation and gave them a task: I asked them to make flags.

They took the remnants of the worn hymnals and created strings of bunting, with each flag made from a cherished song of our congregation. We hung them on Easter Sunday, and people walked into a room with words of worship and blessing strung from our ceiling in an array of hope and delight.

As the service ended, I gave out the remaining pages of the books to all those gathered, along with some scissors, tape, and wooden barbecue skewers I had bought from a dollar store. "Easter," I said to my church family, "reminds us that things that seem dead can have new life. It reminds us that there is hope for new things." I invited them to go through the hymnals and rescue their favorite words. "Make a flag," I told them. And everyone did.

I had asked the musicians ahead of time to sing a song of resurrection, the words of which talk about Christ rising from the dead. After they had sung a couple of verses, I had planned to gently *suggest* that people could wave their flags as we sang the rest of the song. We're not exactly a flag-waving church, so I knew it was a little risky. I was fully prepared for the flags to stay put in people's pockets and purses.

Once again, I should have guessed what would happen next; once again, I didn't. It turned out I didn't need to ask them to wave the flags. When the first notes of the music swelled, the flags were high in the air, every one of them, sweeping back and forth in praise and purpose. Flags that said, "Amazing Grace," and "My Jesus I Love Thee," and "Blessed Assurance, Jesus Is Mine." Those hymnals hadn't been useful for a long time; they would have been garbage to most. But they found a new purpose, as flags of resurrection hope.

That's redemption, the thing for which we learn to make room. Making room for redemption means making room for something good to come from our bad. Room for redemption is the space to trust that there can still be new stories to tell, new songs to sing, and new flags to wave.

We make room to say, one day, "Thank you, God, that the worst thing wasn't the last thing. *And* you always have something new for us."

If you are grieving, it may seem that there can be no good from your story of loss, no light in the darkness. But I invite you to make even the littlest bit of room for redemption. I encourage you to make space, when you are ready, for new stories, new beginnings, new light. I ask you to trust that, one day, you will do things you thought impossible. That you will walk where you thought you could not walk—that you will move forward, one foot in front of the other, and discover new places to arrive, where you never thought you would be.

Making room for redemption means making room for the hope that you will not just get through your grief but that there can be ways that you will become a version of yourself that you will be glad to be. Room for redemption gives space for what you don't think is possible.

I never thought that I would be able to officiate a marriage for a sister on life support on that day in 2014.

I never thought grief support would be one of the most significant parts of my ministry.

I never thought I would ever move forward.

I never saw who I would become on the other side of grief: different, changed, and, yes, redeemed.

I never thought that, one day, you'd be reading my redemption story.

One day, I hope you'll discover your own redemption story to share.

ANOTHER INTRODUCTION

I am thirty-six years old. I have been asked to speak at a conference about where we find God in the midst of darkness. I know I need to talk about where I found light as Roxanne died. I sing the blessing song I sang over Roxanne as she was dying, repeating it several times throughout the talk. At the end, we are all singing, "The Lord bless you and keep you," four hundred people together. I feel God in the valley, present in this beautiful thin space.

I'm thirty-nine years old, and a congregant asks me out for coffee. She tells me that her sister is dying. She tells me that she doesn't know how to tell people, that she doesn't know how to get through the next year, but she feels she can reach out to me because she knows I also lost a sister. She knows I will make room for dying when she needs it.

I am forty-one, and as I'm walking through my neighborhood, I see a friend whose mother just died. We sit on her porch, and we talk for an hour. "I wanted to reach out to you," she says. "I knew I would be able to talk to you. I knew you would understand." Room for the grief bubble, on a porch on a warm summer night.

I am forty-two years old, and for the seventh Christmas in a row, my children are sitting around me as I read *The House of Wooden Santas*. They are thirteen and ten now, and they still make sure I don't miss a single night. I have grown to love this book, this tradition. It turns out it is a beautiful story without my grief-rage. I'm so glad I made room to try this story again, room for a new ritual that honors Roxanne year after year.

My child, Lucy Roxanne, is eight years old, and she comes home from her school Christmas store with all her money spent. "How did you spend twenty dollars at a school Christmas store?" I ask her, baffled. Most items are a dollar or less, and her Christmas list was just our family of four. She only took a twenty because we couldn't find change. Lucy starts to list all the kids she gave a gift to, how at the end, she had one dollar left and realized a friend she missed, so she gave them her last dollar. I laugh, knowing Roxanne would have done the exact same thing. I wish Roxanne could have known this miniature version of herself, wish Lucy could have known the aunt who loved her so well. I make room for regret, room to remember, and room to still carry my loss.

I'm thirty-six and it is just a year after Roxanne has died. I have a dream. I am sitting, and Roxanne comes to me, takes my hands. I look at her, see her peaceful, tumor-free face, a beautiful body renewed. "Oh, Roxanne," I say, "it's been *so* hard." I cry. "I know, my love," Roxanne replies, full of gentle compassion. We hug. I wake up. I feel full of peace. I never thought I'd take such solace in a dream, but I've taken room to reconsider—and I know this is a gift.

I am forty-three, and Roxanne's daughters, Emily and Hannah, are at my house for dinner, as they are every Wednesday. I still pinch myself that Hannah got a job in the next city over and Emily decided to do a master's program here. It is the joy of my life, having them so close, the gift from God that I never even dared to ask for. Hannah and Lucy, now in piano lessons herself, move to the keyboard, and Hannah suggests they play a duet. Emily stands behind them, and the three of them start to sing. Oh, my heart. Could this gift be any sweeter? I never could have dreamed there could be room for resurrection to look like this, for midweek dinners and after-supper sing-alongs to continue in my own house with another generation.

I am forty-four, and I am writing a book because I have a story to share, one I didn't want. But I have done it. I have written it. And I can hear Roxanne's voice: "Don't forget, Leanne. Show right off."

I whisper to her that I will. I will keep telling her story. I will make room for redemption, again and again and again.

REFLECTIONS, PRACTICES, AND PRAYERS

These reflection questions, practices, and prayers, organized by chapter, can be used for your individual reflection or as discussion guides and activities in a small group. If you are using this guide on your own, you can simply pause and consider responses in your mind, or you may find it helpful to journal about them. Please skip anything that doesn't feel helpful—for example, the prayers may not connect with your spiritual or religious expressions, or a practice may not be helpful in a particular season of your grief. Use only what resonates with you.

1 ROOM TO BE UNCERTAIN

REFLECTION

- What were some of the things you worried about most as you faced your loved one dying or processed their death?
- Why do you think people tell us that we should "think positive" when we face hard things? Do you find this helpful? Why or why not?
- Have you ever felt like the father in the story from Scripture who prayed, "I do believe, help me overcome my unbelief"? How so?
- What are you struggling to believe right now? What do you find easy to believe? How can you have room for both?

REFLECTIONS, PRACTICES, AND PRAYERS

PRACTICE: NAMING OUR FEARS

This activity is about saying your biggest fears out loud. Take several pieces of paper, and on each one, write something that you fear as you think about your grief or your experience of your loved one being sick or dying.

After you have written all you can think of, take each paper, one at a time, and read what you wrote out loud.

If you are in a group, put all the papers in one basket. After everyone has placed their papers in the basket, pass them around, taking turns drawing a piece of paper and reading what is written on it out loud. This way, people can hear their fears read out loud without having to say them themselves.

Take a few moments to discuss or reflect on how you experienced this activity.

PRAYER

Dear God,

I struggle to hold on to faith right now. Things do not make as much sense as they once did. They are not as clear as they once were. I long for understanding and fear it will never come. I do believe. Help me overcome my unbelief.

Amen.

2 ROOM FOR THE "AND"

REFLECTION

- Leanne shared about her sister's appointment at the cancer clinic, which included one of her favorite and one of her hardest memories with Roxanne. Do you have examples of experiences like this, when awful times also held cherished moments?
- What were some of the good memories that surrounded the death or dying of your loved one? When were times that you laughed?
- Why can it be difficult to accept that two seemingly opposite things can be true? (example: I am sad and happy. I am angry and relieved.)
- How does it help to embrace "and" as we are grieving?
- What are some of the contrasting emotions you've felt at the same time as you've grieved?

PRACTICE: MAKING ROOM FOR THE "AND"

Take a piece of paper and make two columns. In one column, write difficult or hard emotions you have had as you've grieved (examples: sadness, rage). In the second column, write things that are positive or easier emotions (examples: happiness, gratitude). After you are done, write the word "and" between each set of two words in the columns. Read the newly formed sentences out loud, saying, "I felt..." or "I feel..." Your sentences will sound something like, "I feel sadness *and* happiness" or "I feel rage *and* gratitude.

How does it feel to know all these feelings can coexist?

PRAYER

Dear God,

I am broken and healing, angry and peaceful, bitter and grate-ful. I am sad and I laugh sometimes. I feel battered, and I still wake up each day. I'm uncertain and still trying to believe. I am struggling, and I am trying. Be with me, and remind me that while the emotions are big, I will not be consumed.

Amen.

3 ROOM FOR THE GRIEF TO COME

REFLECTION

- Many people do not get the opportunity to share or reflect on the experiences leading up to a death. If your loved one had a death you knew was coming, what were some of the experiences you had as you prepared for their death?
- What was the most meaningful experience in that season? What was the most difficult?
- Did you find it encouraging or frustrating if people focused on your loved one being healed? Or a mix of both? Why?
- What kind of space did you need as your loved one was dying? What was most helpful in that season? What was not helpful? What do you wish had been different?
- Leanne mentioned common tasks of the season of dying, such as planning a funeral; writing a eulogy; managing food donations, visitors, and different responses of people who want to help; and moving to palliative care. What were the tasks you found most difficult? Why were they important?
- If you are a Christian or a person of faith, how can you hold on to the hope of heaven while also acknowledging the tragedy of death?

PRACTICE: REPLACING THE CLICHÉS

Brainstorm and list all the clichés you heard or have heard in seasons when people are dying. Examples might include: "God only takes the best." "God must have wanted another flower for heaven's garden." "They're in a better place." "At least their suffering is over."

You can write these on pieces of paper, or you can write them on an erasable whiteboard. If you are on your own, pause to consider those that were not helpful for you. Tear them up or erase them. If you are in a group, discuss together what was helpful and not help-ful. Destroy (tear up or erase) the clichés that did not make room for dying.

Now share what phrases you could use to replace these clichés. What words have others spoken to you that have meant a lot? What other-than-verbal gestures could replace the clichés?

PRAYER

Dear God,

To you who knew the reality of impending death and wept tears of blood in the garden of Gethsemane, we give the hurts, frus-trations, and regrets that we experienced as our loved one died.

Amen.

4 ROOM IN THE VALLEY OF DEATH

REFLECTION

- Where have you experienced the things Leanne mentioned in this chapter during seasons of death and/or grieving?
  - Indecisiveness: Did you struggle with decisions? How so?
  - Helplessness: Did you feel helpless? Why or why not? What did it look like for you?
  - Desperation: How did you or others experience feeling desperate?
  - Normal Life: Did it surprise you that life continued while you were surrounded by death? What was that like?
  - Suffering: How did you experience this?
- As you look back at the time your loved one was dying or in your season of grief, where did you feel the "staff" of God? Where did you find comfort?
- Where did you experience things like a "rod?" Where did things feel painful?
- As you think about the "shadow" of death, looking back, can you see places where God or hope was present?
- Do you believe that death and dying can be a "thin place?" Why or why not?

PRACTICE: EXPERIENCING A GUIDED MEDITATION

This is a guided reflection of remembering the most difficult season of your grieving. It can be led by someone in a group, or you can read it on your own. Either way, read it slowly, taking time to pause, take deep breaths, and let yourself or others feel what is needed. If you are doing this in a group, remember that others are with you; if you are doing it by yourself, remember that others are doing this practice elsewhere.

Close your eyes and picture yourself in a deep valley. Large mountains loom around you, and you see no path out of the valley. For now, you are alone. Ominous clouds fill the sky, casting a dark shadow over the whole valley. You cannot see any rays of sun.

Think of this valley as your own darkest place of your grieving season. For a few moments, let yourself remember the emotions of that time. Remember being in the darkest place. You may remember the valley of the hospice room. Or the funeral home.

What are you feeling? What sounds are around you? What images are coming to mind?

What are you wishing would be different in this moment? Where are the people you care about? What do you most long for?

Now picture that you are not *alone. I want you to consider that God is there in the valley.*

What is God doing in the valley with you? How do you feel God? Are you aware that God is there? Why or why not? Pause now, and picture God's hand on your shoulder.

Pause again and picture God pausing and sitting next to you, God taking your hand.

What do you want to say to God in this valley? Is it something about how hard it is or how much it hurts? How does God respond?

Give a few moments for people or for yourself to sit and process, and then read Psalm 23. When everyone is done, anyone who wants to can share what they have experienced. (If you are leading this exercise, please note that this may be very raw for many, so give space for a range of emotions.)

PRAYER

Dear God,

The shadow is sometimes so extensive that I can see nothing but darkness. But you tell us that you are with us in the shadows. Help me to remember that you are with me, even in the bleakest times and places.

Amen.

5 ROOM FOR IMPERFECT GOODBYES

REFLECTION

- Before your loved one died, how would you have described the "perfect" goodbye at the end of someone's life?
- Where did most of your images of dying come from? Were most of them from movies or books? How did this shape your thoughts on what last moments should look like?
- How did you feel about your loved one's death? What was hardest about it?
- Were there things that you felt cheated out of in the way your goodbye did or did not happen?
- Share what happened when your loved one died, if you feel ready (you can do this in a group, or find someone you trust to share with if you are on your own, or journal).

PRACTICE: MAKING ROOM FOR GOODBYES

Make room for things to which you want to say goodbye. If you are able, get some sand, and place it in a shallow plate or bowl. If you are near a beach, you can walk to a beach and use sand there, or use dirt from your garden or a local park. With a stick or your finger, list the words that you wish to let go. Give yourself time to do this. After each word, wipe them away, and write a new one.

You can also do this activity using Scrabble tiles or block letters. Make the words you need to release out of these tiles, and then shake up the tiles so the word disappears.

Other options include: an Etch A Sketch, a whiteboard or window with dry-erase markers, or a chalkboard and eraser.

PRAYER

Dear God,

Into your hands I commit that which is so hard to let go. As I say goodbye, fill the empty places that feel left behind with hope and healing.

Amen.

6 ROOM FOR THE RITUALS

REFLECTION

- Did you have a funeral or memorial service for your loved one? Why or why not?
- How are you feeling about that decision after reading this chapter?
- If you had a service, what was most meaningful to you about it? What things would you change?
- Why do you think cultures have so many funeral and grieving rituals? What role do they play?
- Why do we want to skip them?
- If you did decide to skip a ritual as you grieved, what would it look like to include it now?

PRACTICE: WRITING A EULOGY

It might be that you got to share a eulogy already, but you may not have. Take one page of paper and fill in a eulogy for your loved one. If you need help, complete these sentences. (Please note this works for those with a good relationship with the person they lost, but may be hard for those with complicated grief. A second option for that is on the next page.)

My loved one was special to me because _____.
One of my favorite memories with them is _____.
Another one is _____. Some of the things they loved best were _____. A really cool thing about them is that _____. Here's another thing that's cool about them: _____. I'm going to really miss _____.
This is something that they taught me: _____. I will honor them by _____.

For a complicated situation.

The relationship I had with my person was _____.
Many things were complicated, such as _____. But
I also try to think of good things about them. A good trait that they
had was _____. One thing that is a good or positive
memory is _____. But I wish _____ had
been different. I wish that they knew _____. One thing
that I learned from this relationship is _____. And
something that I will do differently in my life because of them is
_____.

Share your eulogies with your group, or read them to or send them
to someone you care about.

PRAYER

Dear God,

Thank you for the time I got to have _____ in
my life. Thank you that their life was important, in its own
way. Thank you that it is okay to honor their life and mark
their death.

Amen.

7 ROOM FOR THE GRIEF BUBBLE

REFLECTION

- Do you resonate with the idea of being in a grief bubble? Why or why not?
- What has the grief bubble been like for you?
- What is like it to be around other people as you are grieving?
- What is an example of a time that you felt especially separated or distant from others by grief?
- What did/do you find hardest to do when you were/are in the grief bubble?
- What do you wish people understood about it?
- How can we help other people understand the grief bubble?

PRACTICE: IMAGINING THE GRIEF BUBBLE

Take a piece of paper and draw yourself in the center (Yes, a stick person is fine!). Then draw a bubble (circle) around yourself, leaving lots of room outside the bubble on the paper.

On the paper, write or draw all the things that feel distant from you right now in the space outside your bubble. Discuss this with your group, or journal about it.

When you are done, consider what you would draw *inside* your bubble. What people, ideas, or feelings are in the bubble? Discuss or journal about this.

PRAYER

Dear God,

I so often feel like I am all alone. I feel like people do not and cannot understand. I feel like it is just me and my grief and like it will never be anything more than that. When I am in the bubble, help me remember that you are still carrying me, bubble and all.

Amen.

8 ROOM TO NOT HAVE ROOM

REFLECTION

- Have you noticed that you have less energy and capacity when you are grieving?
- If so, how have you discovered that grief makes you tired?
- What are some of the activities you once enjoyed that you have struggled to enjoy while grieving?
- What do you think of the idea of scheduling "grief time"? Where could you fit grief time in your schedule?
- How can we help others understand the way grief impacts us in this way?

PRACTICE: MAKING ROOM IN YOUR FULL GLASS

On a piece of paper, draw a picture of a glass. Write all the things in your glass that take up your life and schedule. Think of as many as you can. These may include things like family, driving kids to practices, committees, work projects, and so on.

When you are done, consider: Knowing that grief takes up so much room in our "glasses," what can you take out of your glass in this season to give yourself some room? Even if it is difficult, try to think of at least one area you can give yourself permission to let go.

If you are in a group, brainstorm together ways each person can make space in their schedule. (Can they hire a cleaner? Can they ask for time off work? Can they ask for help in certain areas?)

How will you communicate to others your decision to give yourself this space for grief?

PRAYER

Dear God,

I so often feel at the brink, with life and with grief. My to-do list feels so long that I don't always know where my grief can fit. Help me to take the space I need to grieve, and remove any guilt I feel for needing more room for me right now.

Amen.

9 ROOM FOR PEOPLE TO LET YOU DOWN

REFLECTION

- Have you experienced hurt from people who did not support you as you have needed while you were grieving? What has that been like?
- What has been the hardest relationship for you to manage during your loss?
- What has been the most painful thing someone said to you?
- Do you believe it is possible to live with "open hands," which can allow others to make mistakes while we are grieving? Why or why not?
- In this chapter, Leanne suggests that it is not just the role of other people to "do better" when it comes to helping us but also our role to learn to forgive. Do you agree or disagree? Why would forgiveness be important?
- Are there ways that grief can help us realize relationships that are not good for us? Is it okay to lose some relationships because of our grief?
- Is there a relationship you would like to see healed that was harmed as a result of grief? What would it look like to seek healing in that relationship for you?

PRACTICE: CONSIDERING THE THIRDS

Make a chart with three columns. In the first column, list names of people who helped you in your grief. In the second column, list those who have been neutral—neither helpful nor hurtful. In the third column, list those who have felt hurtful. Note that the same person may appear in more than one column. After you finish your list, consider the following:

- What do you notice about your list?
- Are some people in more than one column?
- Are some columns longer than others? Why or why not?

As you look at the list of those who have been helpful, consider how you can express your thanks to them.

As you look at those who have been hurtful, consider what it would look like to process that hurt. Do any of these relationships matter deeply to you? If you want to keep these people in your life, consider:

- Do you need to have a conversation with anyone on this list to share your hurt?
- Do you need to let things go?
- Do you need to offer forgiveness?

PRAYER

Dear God,

For the people who have helped give me grieving room, I thank you, with gratitude. For the people who have been neutral in my life, I acknowledge that they remain important to me. For those who have hurt me, I ask for wisdom to know the next steps, grace to have hard conversations, and strength to forgive if necessary.

Amen.

10 ROOM FOR THE ROLLER COASTER

REFLECTION

- Have you ever believed that grief progressed through stages? Why did you think this?
- How has your grief looked like a roller coaster?
- Do you find it comforting or discouraging (or a mix of both) to think that your grief is like a roller coaster instead of a steady uphill journey? Why?
- Have you ever experienced a "grief burst?" Share what happened.

PRACTICE: LOOKING FOR PATTERNS

On a piece of paper in landscape position, draw a timeline of the last year or few months, creating a horizontal line along the paper, with the name of each month listed every couple of inches. Place dots over and above the line to indicate "high" and "low" dates of your grief. For example, for an anniversary, you might put a dot way below the line. For a vacation where you felt pretty good, you might place the dot above the line. Connect the dots when you are done, creating your own "roller coaster" image. Look for the patterns of highs and lows, even as you acknowledge the unpredictable nature of grief.

Discuss with others or reflect:

- What do you notice about your own roller coaster?
- What things seemed to trigger the hardest times of your grief?
- What does this image teach you about how grief works?

PRAYER

Dear God,

Please be with me in the ups, the downs, and the plateaus of the roller coaster. Help me survive the lowest lows and be thankful for the highest highs. Remind me that you are holding me safe as I live the ride of grief.

Amen.

11 ROOM FOR REGRET

REFLECTION

- What are some of the regrets you carry as you think of your loved one?
- What are things that you especially regret that you will not get to see or experience with them?
- Why do you think is it so difficult to name our regrets?
- Do you agree that we should live without regret? Why and how is regret okay?
- What would you do differently if you could, looking back on your relationship with your loved one?

PRACTICE: COLLECTING WISHES

If you are doing this in a group, gather as many pennies, or coins, or coin-like objects as you can. Give everyone in the group a handful. Have a bowl or bucket of water ready to become a "wishing well." Go around the room, with each person in turn naming a statement starting with "I wish," expressing a regret they have in terms of their lost loved one. (Some examples: "I wish we had tried another treatment," "I wish I had called them the day they died," "I wish I could see them grow up.") Each time someone makes a "wish," they can drop a penny into the water.

If you are on your own, you can still create your own "wishing well" and do this by yourself. You could also try this activity with other "wishing" actions, such as blowing out a candle or blowing the petals off a dandelion. Write or say as many "I wish" statements as you need.

PRAYER

Dear God,

There is so much that I regret, so much that I wish was different. I regret things said and unsaid, actions taken and things left undone. I regret that the future looks different than I hoped it would and that the past is so complicated. I name to you my regrets and ask you to help me carry them.

Amen.

12 ROOM FOR RAGE

REFLECTION

- Have you ever experienced "grief-rage?" When did it happen? What did it look like?
- Do you consider anger a negative emotion? Do you think it's wrong or bad to be angry? Why or why not?
- Why do you think grief make us angry?
- In this chapter, Leanne talked about a woman who said she realized that she wasn't really mad at people who behaved unhelpfully; she was mad that her grandchild had died. What do you think of this? Have you ever experienced this in your life? How do you now see that your anger was because of grief?
- How do we cope with our grief-rage? How can we make space for healthy anger?
- How can we know when our anger is unhealthy for us? What do we do when our anger feels out of control?

PRACTICE: GRABBING A TENNIS RACKET

Go to a thrift store and purchase an old tennis racket or badminton racket. If this is difficult, you can use a stick or an other simple-to-destroy item. As a group, or on your own, take your item and find a safe space to smash it to pieces.

Each time you smash the item, yell or scream (yes, really yell!) something you are angry about. In a group, you can take turns passing the racket around to smash, one turn at a time.

This activity may be outside of some people's comfort zones. An alternative can simply be to say your reasons for anger out loud, without using a racket.

PRAYER

Dear God,

I feel so angry that they died. Each day I feel the injustice of it all, and sometimes I feel that my anger has no place to go. Protect others from my misplaced anger, and protect me from rage that would harm me or my relationships. Help me remember, too, that it is okay that I am mad. Hold me, and hold my anger.

Amen.

13 ROOM FOR HARD HOLIDAYS (AND OTHER DAYS THAT SUCK)

REFLECTION

- What days or seasons of the year were, or still are, hardest for you? Why?
- Are there times that felt difficult that you did not anticipate would be hard?
- Many grievers share that sometimes the days leading up to the holiday or anniversary are harder than the day itself. Have you ever found this in your life? How so?
- How do you cope on hard days? What strategies can help us survive?
- Are there days or holidays coming up that you are afraid to face? What are they? What will make them challenging?
- What might help you get through those hard days? How can you communicate what you need to your other loved ones?
- How can you add new traditions or modify old ones to make hard days more manageable?

PRACTICE: WRITING A LETTER

Make a copy of the letter Leanne wrote about grieving at Christmas by typing it out or handwriting your own version. In your letter, fill in your own hard holidays and make changes to make it your own. What days would you change or add to this letter? What requests would you take out? What would you change? What would you add?

If a hard holiday is coming up in your life, send this letter to those that care about you, or share it online.

PRAYER

Dear God,

Be with me in my hardest days and hardest nights and hardest seasons. When I struggle to feel cheerful on days that once held joy, remind me that it is okay to take grieving room, even at times when it feels there is no space for my sadness.

Amen.

14 ROOM TO TALK ABOUT IT

REFLECTION

- Why do you think many of us find it difficult to talk about our grief?
- Do you find it easy or difficult to talk about your grief? Why or why not?
- Have you tried grief counseling? Did it help? Why or why not?
- What are things that people say that shut us down when we want to talk?
- How do you identify people that really want to listen?
- Leanne talks about two lies she believed when she was grieving: "There's no one to talk to" and "It's too late." Do you agree or disagree that these aren't true? Why or why not?

PRACTICE: FINDING THE SAFE PEOPLE

In this chapter, Leanne talks about "safe people"—people with whom we can be honest about our grief, even years after a loss. Many of us may think that we just don't have such people in our lives. Today, we are going to try to identify safe people.

In each of the following categories, list all the people who come to mind who might be safe people. You could consider people who have shown support, have offered encouragement, or had grief experiences that may help them understand. Who are people who have said (even if it was a long time ago), "If you need anything, I'm here"? Ask yourself, "Who do I trust? Who has been through grief themselves and may understand?" Some examples might include:

- Your immediate family
- Your extended family (cousins, in-laws, aunts, uncles, and others)
- Current friends
- Friends from years past
- Neighbors
- Coworkers and colleagues
- People in your various circles: places you volunteer, clubs you are a part of, your place of worship
- Pastors, counselors, therapists, support groups
- People on social media

Remember, your "safe people" don't have to be close to you. You may even find that the people you love the most are not the right people for you to talk about grief with (even if they try their best).

From all the people that you listed, did you find one or two names of people with whom you can share about your grief? How can you reach out to them when you need it?

PRAYER

Dear God,

You give us the gift of other people to help us. Help me to recognize and trust the people in my life that will be gifts to me to help me process my grief.

Amen.

15 ROOM FOR LAMENT

REFLECTION

- What do you think of the word *lament*? What comes to mind when you hear it?
- Why does our culture struggle with lament? Why is it hard for us to let things be sad without trying to make them better?
- How have you felt when people try to "make you feel better" when you are grieving, with platitudes or assurances that everything will be okay? Why? Why do you think churches and communities of faith struggle to make space for lament?
- Why do you think many people are uncomfortable hearing unresolved stories? What might we do to become more comfortable with them?
- What would it look like for our faith communities to make more room for lament?
- What have you needed to lament as you have grieved? What feels like the saddest pieces of your story?

PRACTICE: NOTING OUR LAMENTS

This practice includes writing down laments on small pieces of paper. Leanne mentioned this activity, which she did with her church; you can also do this with a group or as an individual. On each piece of paper, write something you lament, using as many pieces of paper as you need.

If you are doing this with a group of Christians, you can lay all these papers at a cross (there may be one in your church, or you could draw one or bring one to use in your space). Or you could simply lay these papers on a hearth, or a mantle, or somewhere that makes you think of leaving them with something or someone bigger than yourself. Save the papers to use in the practice for chapter 18.

PRAYER

Dear God,

I am sad. I am angry. I am disappointed. My person died, and the world feels unfair and unsafe. I don't know how I will get through this. I often feel lost and alone. It is hard to see any good in this. Everything sucks.

Amen.

16 ROOM TO RECONSIDER

REFLECTION

- Before your loved one died, what were some of the things that you thought were "easy" to believe? (Example: "Everything happens for a reason" or "Things will work out in the end.") What beliefs that you once held have changed since your person died?
- What has most shaken your faith in God, goodness, or the universe as a result of your loved one's death?
- If you are a person of another faith, have you felt like a bad Christian or Muslim or Jewish person for having questions about how God allowed this to happen? Why or why not?
- What resonated with you in this chapter?

PRACTICE: MAKING SPACE TO RECONSIDER

Make space to explore new understandings of faith with a few options to explore on your own.

- Set up a meeting with a pastor or faith leader you trust, and bring a list of your biggest questions to discuss. Don't hold back.
- If you are a Christian, visit a church of a completely different tradition than yours. Consider the ways it helps you see God in a new way.
- Read the book *Everything Happens for a Reason: And Other Lies I've Loved* by Kate Bowler. Find someone else with whom you can talk about it.
- Let yourself listen to sad songs (on repeat is okay too).
- Read Lamentations from the Bible, making space for a faith that is sad, angry, and outraged.

- Spend a week reading what Walter Bruggeman calls the "Psalms of Disorientation": Psalm 13, Psalm 35, Psalm 74, Psalm 86, Psalm 95, and Psalm 137. On day seven, write your own.

PRAYER

Dear God,

I'm not totally sure what I believe anymore, about you, or my faith, or how things work. But I think that might be okay, and I think you will be with me—and for that, I thank you.

Amen.

17 ROOM FOR YOUR LOVED ONE

REFLECTION

- What are some of your favorite memories of your person? What do you remember about them? Some ideas to prompt your memories: What was their laugh like? How did they smell? Did they have a special perfume or cologne? What was the sound of their voice like? How did they walk? What were some of their favorite things? What drove you crazy about them? What is something that you learned from them? How did they impact your life?
- If you had a difficult relationship or unresolved relationship with the one who died, these questions may be complicated. You might consider: Is there one positive thing you wish to take from them? What lessons will you take from them, even if they were difficult ones?
- Has anyone made you feel like you should stop feeling connected to your loved one? What was that like?
- What could you say to someone who tells you that you should stop remembering them?
- What are things you have done that have helped you remember your person well?

PRACTICE: MOLDING YOUR MEMORIES

This activity is sometimes used as part of therapeutic approaches relying on the "continuing bonds" theory of grief. You can use this on your own, and it can be led in a group with others. (This is a good activity for children trying to process their connection to a lost loved one.)

Take a small handful of two different colors of clay or playdough, one in each hand. One color represents you, and the other color represents the person who died. Now squeeze them together into one piece, and begin blending them together. As you do, consider all the ways that your life was connected to your loved one. Remember all the connections that you have, all the ways that they changed you, and all the things that you shared together. Take as long as you want, reflecting and remembering as you continue to create one piece of clay from the two colors.

When you are ready, consider: Can you separate the two colors of clay? Why not? In the same way, the bond that you have with your loved one can never be broken. Your lives are intertwined, and the connection cannot be undone. You may wish to shape the clay into a shape that is meaningful to you to keep.

PRAYER

Dear God,

Thank you for _____. I thank you for their presence in my life and for the person they were. Thank you for the memories I have of them. Thank you for the ways they will always be with me. Thank you that our relationship can continue for the rest of my life.

Amen.

18 ROOM FOR RESURRECTION

REFLECTION

- Have you ever heard the expression "Bad things come in threes?" Why do you think people say this? Why can this feel comforting in some ways?
- When your person died, did other difficult things happen that added to your grief? What happened?
- How do we process these times of "tragedy upon tragedy"?
- At first, the accident seemed like the worst thing that could have happened to Leanne's family, but later she realized that it helped her family discover that they could move forward in a new way. Leanne calls this "room for resurrection." What do you think of this idea?
- What might it look like to make space for the idea that there can still be new life for you, even in little ways?
- Contemplate the idea from Frederick Buechner: "The resurrection means the worst thing is never the last thing." What might that mean for you?

PRACTICE: MAKING RESURRECTION CONFETTI

Take the papers that you wrote laments on from chapter 15. As Leanne mentioned she did with the lament papers from her church, take time to cut those papers into small, confetti-sized pieces.

Take the confetti pieces in your hands and pray for new hope for resurrection.

On a day or in a place where you want to remember resurrection, you can throw your "confetti." You may want to scatter the pieces on your loved one's grave, remembering the hope of new life, or throw them in the water, or even bury them. Do what works for you. (Please note that it is okay if you are not ready to do this yet. This may take some time for many of us, so be gentle with yourself.)

PRAYER

Dear God,

It so often feels like my worst thing will be the end of me. I cannot always see hope for resurrection around me. When I'm ready, show me that there can still be hope for me.

Amen.

19 ROOM TO NEVER GET OVER IT

REFLECTION

- Has anyone ever asked you, "Are you over it yet?" or something similar? How did you feel about that question? How did you respond? Why is that question often so hurtful?
- What do you think people mean when they talk about "getting over it"? Why do you think people assume that's something we should do?
- What does "not getting over it" mean? Is it a bad thing to continue to carry our grief? Why or why not?
- What ways do the people you know continue to carry and remember their loved one?

PRACTICE: CHOOSING TO REMEMBER

Consider ways that you could continue to make space for your grief and for your loved one. Here are some ideas. Choose one or more that you want to try—or come up with your own.

- Talk about them in daily conversation.
- Commemorate their birthday each year.
- Place a special portrait or picture of them somewhere in your home.
- Wear a memorial piece of jewelry.
- Visit their grave.
- Set up a memorial fund or activity in their honor.
- Play their favorite song, or watch their favorite movie on certain days.
- Create a book of photos and memories about them to share with others (especially children who may not have had a chance to know them).
- Write your story and share it.

- Let yourself cry whenever you need to.
- Tell people when something reminds you of your person.

PRAYER

Dear God,

I know that I will always be a little different than I would have been because of this loss. Help me to remember that that's okay.

Amen.

20 ROOM FOR REDEMPTION

REFLECTION

- What does the word *redemption* mean to you?
- Do you think it's reasonable to hope for redemption from what happened to you? Why or why not?
- What about if nothing "good" ever comes from your loss?
- Leanne says that redemption doesn't mean that you think it's a good thing that the death happened; it means that new things might still come from it. Do you agree? Can we say that the death was bad and also make space for ways good things happened as a result?
- What kind of redemption do you find yourself longing for?

PRACTICE: MAKING A FLAG OF HOPE

Create your own redemption flag. This flag can include words or images that remind you of ways that you have already seen new hope or where you hope you will. If you are doing this in a group, make sure someone brings the items Leanne mentioned in this chapter: you'll need paper, tape, scissors, and markers. Be as creative as you want about the shape of your flag and the words or pictures that it holds.

You might end by gently waving your flags together as a group or on your own. You may also need to bring your flag home and wave it another time, when you're ready.

PRAYER

Dear God,

Thank you for new flags and new beginnings. Help me remember that my worst thing will not be my last thing. Lord, in your mercy, hear my prayer.

Amen.

ACKNOWLEDGMENTS

"Thank you" seems too simple a statement to fully express the depth of gratitude I feel to everyone who helped *Grieving Room* come to be. To each of you, know that this thanks comes with deep love, gratitude, and respect.

Thank you to Sam Loaker and Kevin Makins, who pushed me to write the book you were certain I should share. I believe this book would not exist without either of you.

Thank you to Leslie Makins and James Bowick, who read the very first version of this manuscript and provided invaluable insight that helped shape what this book needed to be. (And, yes, you were right about everything.)

Thank you to my early readers, who assured me that this project was worth pursuing and helped make it better: Dwight Friesen, Sherri Gunther-Trautwein, Sharlene MacLennan, George Montague, Jill Coombs, and Jan Reid-Evaleigh. I appreciate you all.

Thank you to Amanda De Santis and Colleen Gleadall, who helped me establish my "Grieving Room" Instagram page, which ended up helping this book find a publisher. Thank you to Mariah Loaker, for your help with graphic design, and Dawn Danko, for the gift of your photography skills.

Thank you to my agent, Don Pape, for being willing to take a risk on a new author, and thank you to Ellen Graf-Martin, for introducing us. Thank you to Valerie Weaver-Zercher and the whole team at Broadleaf Books, for your wisdom and support.

Thank you to my cherished family, who have been encouraging and supportive of this project. To "Hannah" and "Emily"—thank

ACKNOWLEDGMENTS

you for letting me share your mom's story and for being the best ever Hamilton Fam Jam. Dallas, thank you for believing in me and making everything I try to do better. I love you. Thank you to Josiah and Lucy, for sharing me with this project and giving me so much room to live out all my callings. I love you beyond measure.

Thank you to all the congregants of Mount Hamilton Baptist Church. Thank you for sharing your hearts, your stories, and your lives with me. Thank you for carrying me through my grief and for the constant support and encouragement to make grief support a part of my ministry. I will always be grateful for the grieving room you gave to me.

Finally, thank you to everyone who let me share their stories and wisdom in this book. I learned so much from all of you.

NOTES

CHAPTER 3

41 *Another author summarizes it this way*: Austin H. Kutsher, "Anticipatory Grief, Death, and Bereavement: A Continuum," in *Phenomenon of Death: Faces of Mortality*, ed. Edith Wyschogrod (New York: Harper & Row, 1973).

CHAPTER 4

55 *David Adam writes about the Celtic church*: David Adam, *Eye of the Eagle* (London: Triangle, 1990), 11.

CHAPTER 6

68 *Amanda Held Opelt speaks to this reality*: Amanda Held Opelt, *A Hole in the World: Finding Hope in Rituals of Grief and Healing* (Brentwood, TN: Worthy Books, 2022), 211.

CHAPTER 7

78 *Christian author C. S. Lewis says in his classic book*: C. S. Lewis, *A Grief Observed* (London: Faber & Faber, 1961), 5.

86 *In her seminal grief work*: Megan Devine, *It's OK That You're Not OK: Meeting Grief and Loss in a Culture That Doesn't Understand* (Louisville, CO: Sounds True, 2017), 1.

NOTES

CHAPTER 9

97　*In Understanding Your Grief, grief expert Alan Wolfelt*: Alan D. Wolfelt, *Understanding Your Grief: Ten Essential Touchstones for Finding Hope and Healing Your Heart* (Fort Collins, CO: Companion Press, 2003), 127–28.

CHAPTER 10

101　*Many people get this idea*: E. Kübler-Ross, *On Death and Dying* (New York: Macmillan, 1969).

103　*Alan Wolfelt describes these experiences as*: Wolfelt, *Understanding Your Grief*, 75–76.

CHAPTER 13

131　*Maybe you have your own version*: Leanne Friesen, "On Behalf of the Grieving at Christmas," leannefriesen.com, November 24, 2015, https://leannefriesen.com/2015/11/24/on-behalf-of-the-grieving-at-christmas/.

CHAPTER 14

142　*One thing I recommend is advice*: Susan P. Halpern, *The Etiquette of Illness: What to Say When You Can't Find the Words* (New York: Bloomsbury, 2004).

CHAPTER 15

149　*Biblical scholar Walter Brueggemann labels these*: Walter Brueggemann, *The Spirituality of the Psalms* (Minneapolis: Fortress Press, 2002), 10.

152　*In her book Traveling Mercies*: Anne Lamott, *Traveling Mercies: Some Thoughts on Faith* (New York: Anchor Books, 1999), 70.

CHAPTER 17

165　*C. S. Lewis wrote about it well*: Lewis, *A Grief Observed*, 11.

166 *In 1996 Dennis Klass*: Dennis Klass, Phyllis Silverman, and Steve Nickman, *Continuing Bonds: New Theories of Grief* (New York: Taylor & Francis, 1996).

CHAPTER 18

179 *It read: "I know that*: Lamott, *Traveling Mercies*, 63.